MW00587671

TO BE A
CHRISTIAN

TO BE A
CHRISTIAN

An Anglican Catechism

APPROVED EDITION

WHEATON, ILLINOIS

TO BE A CHRISTIAN: AN ANGLICAN CATECHISM

Copyright © 2020 by The Anglican Church in North America

Published by Crossway
      1300 Crescent Street
      Wheaton, Illinois 60187

Working edition previously released by Anglican House Publishers, 2014

Cover design: Kevin Lipp

First printing 2020

Printed in the United States of America

Hardcover ISBN: 978-1-4335-6677-6
ePub ISBN: 978-1-4335-6680-6
PDF ISBN: 978-1-4335-6678-3
Mobipocket ISBN: 978-1-4335-6679-0

Library of Congress Cataloging-in-Publication Data

Title: To be a Christian: an Anglican catechism.
Description: Approved Edition | Wheaton: Crossway, 2020. | Includes index.
Identifiers: LCCN 2019025495 (print) | LCCN 2019025496 (ebook) | ISBN 9781433566776 (hardcover) | ISBN 9781433566783 (pdf) | ISBN 9781433566790 (mobi) | ISBN 9781433566806 (epub)
Subjects: LCSH: Anglican Communion—Catechisms. | Anglican Communion—Doctrines—Miscellanea.
Classification: LCC BX5005 .T6 2020 (print) | LCC BX5005 (ebook) | DDC 238/.3—dc23
LC record available at https://lccn.loc.gov/2019025495
LC ebook record available at https://lccn.loc.gov/2019025496

Crossway is a publishing ministry of Good News Publishers.

SH		30	29	28	27	26	25	24	23
15	14	13	12	11	10	9	8	7	6	5

TABLE *of* CONTENTS

PREFACE

Why an *Anglican* catechism? Anglicans are heirs of a rich tradition of Christian faith and life. That tradition stretches from today's worldwide Anglican Communion of millions of believers on six continents back centuries to laymen like William Wilberforce, who led the abolition of the slave trade in England, to the bishops and martyrs of the English Reformation like Thomas Cranmer, and to missionaries like Augustine of Canterbury and Saint Patrick, who spread the Gospel throughout the British Isles.

Throughout these centuries, Anglicans have articulated their faith in reference to classic sources of doctrine and worship. All true doctrine, Anglicans believe, is derived from Holy Scripture, which is the wellspring and ground for testing all that is taught in the Church. Saint Paul instructs the Church, "All Scripture is breathed out by God and profitable for teaching, for reproof, for correction, and for training in righteousness" *(2 Timothy 3:16).* Further, Article 6 of the Articles of Religion states, "Whatever is not read therein, nor may be proved thereby, is not to be required of any man that it should be believed as an article of the Faith."

Classic sources for the explication and elucidation of scriptural doctrine include the following:

- *The Early Church.* Anglicans have always held in high regard "such teachings of the ancient Fathers and Councils of the Church as are agreeable to the Scriptures," and which are summarized in the Apostles' Creed, Nicene-Constantinopolitan Creed, and Athanasian Creed.

- *The Articles of Religion (1571)*. The Articles, also known as the "Thirty-Nine Articles," summarize the biblical faith recovered at the Reformation and have become the doctrinal norm for Anglicans around the world.
- *The King James Bible (1611)*. The translation of the Bible into English, begun in the sixteenth century by William Tyndale, achieved its classic form in the 1611 translation under King James I and remains the basis for many modern versions, such as the Revised Standard Version and the English Standard Version. In keeping with the principles of the English Reformation that promote worship in language that the people understand *(Articles of Religion, 24)*, the Bible has since been translated into many languages. Anglican Christianity has now spread to encompass people of many races and languages all over the world.
- *The Book of Common Prayer (1549–1662)*. The Anglican Prayer Book is known worldwide as one of the finest expressions of Christian prayer and worship. The 1662 Prayer Book is predominantly composed of Scriptures formulated into prayer. It has been the standard for Anglican doctrine, discipline, and worship, and for subsequent revisions in many languages.
- *Music and hymnody*. Hymns, from writers like Isaac Watts, Charles Wesley, John Mason Neale, and Graham Kendrick, have formed the spirituality of English-speaking Anglicans around the world. Today, composers in many languages continue in this powerful tradition of catechesis through music.
- *The Lambeth Quadrilateral*. Resolution 11 of the Lambeth Conference (1888) affirmed four marks of Church identity required for genuine unity and fellowship. These are the Holy Scriptures containing "all things necessary for salvation," the Apostles' and Nicene Creeds as "the sufficient statement of the Christian faith," two sacraments ordained

by Christ—Baptism and the Eucharist—and "the historic Episcopate, locally adapted." These serve as a basis of Anglican identity, as well as instruments for ecumenical dialogue with other church traditions.

- *The Jerusalem Declaration (2008)*. This statement from the Global Anglican Future Conference in 2008 has become the theological basis for the Global Fellowship of Confessing Anglicans, of which the Anglican Church in North America is a part.

In keeping with this rich, diverse, and historic tradition of doctrine and worship, we receive this catechism and commend its use for the building up of the Church today.

We envision this catechism being used for courses, shorter or longer, based on groups of questions and answers. The degree to which it is used directly for instruction and the amount of memorization asked of individual catechumens are left to the catechist to determine by context and circumstance. What is more, the resources of modern technology open up multiple possibilities for its use in creative new ways.

A catechism is ideally to be used in the context of a relationship between the catechist (the discipleship instructor) and the catechumen (the one being instructed) to foster the process of catechesis (disciple-making). The catechumen is invited by the catechist to a new identity in Christ and into a new community, to the praise of God's glory, to the practice of stewardship, and to sharing in the ministry of making disciples of all nations.

Building on the 2014 working edition of the catechism, this edition (approved 2018) has been enriched by feedback from hundreds of laypersons, clergy, bishops, and theologians of the Church. This input helped create a catechism we trust will be useful, especially for those raised with limited exposure to the Christian faith.

We give thanks for the sacrificial work and scholarship of those listed below, who have served the Church in the creation of the two editions of this catechism.

We pray that this book will be an effective instrument to disciple believers in the truth of the Gospel, so that they may serve Jesus Christ throughout the world *(2 Timothy 2:15)*. May this catechism serve to build up the Body of Christ by grounding Christian believers in the Gospel.

On behalf of the College of Bishops
of the Anglican Church in North America

The Most Reverend Foley Beach
Archbishop and Primate

The Most Reverend Robert Duncan
Archbishop and Primate, 2009–2014

COMMITTEES, WRITERS, AND CONSULTANTS

THE REVEREND CANON DR. J. I. PACKER
THEOLOGICAL EDITOR

THE REVEREND DR. JOEL SCANDRETT
EXECUTIVE EDITOR

ANGLICAN CHURCH IN NORTH AMERICA COMMITTEE FOR CATECHESIS

Mr. Kirk Botula
Mrs. Taryn Bullis
The Reverend Brian Foos
The Reverend Dr. Jack Gabig
The Reverend Canon Arthur Going
Dr. Philip Harrold
The Reverend Dr. Stephen Lake
Mrs. Kristy Leaseburg
The Reverend Lee Nelson
The Reverend Tripp Prince
The Reverend Ben Roberts
The Reverend Dr. Joel Scandrett
Mrs. Bronwyn Short
Dr. Leslie Thyberg

WRITERS/CONSULTANTS

Mr. Timothy Belcher
The Reverend John Boonzaaijer
The Reverend Dr. Susan Bubbers
The Reverend Dr. Charles Erlandson
The Reverend Randall Foster
The Reverend Mark Galli
Dr. Sarah Lebhar Hall
Dr. Gary Holt
The Reverend Dr. Toby Karlowicz
The Very Reverend Dr. Robert Munday
The Very Reverend Dr. Stephen Noll
Dr. Daniel Olson
The Reverend Canon Dr. J. I. Packer
Dr. Ann Paton
Mrs. Amelia Schmotzer
The Very Reverend Dr. Justyn Terry
Dr. William Witt

ANGLICAN CHURCH IN NORTH AMERICA BISHOPS REVIEW COMMITTEE

The Right Reverend Dr. Bill Atwood
The Most Reverend Dr. Foley Beach
The Right Reverend John Guernsey
The Right Reverend Neil Lebhar
The Right Reverend Dr. Francis Lyons
The Right Reverend Dr. Eric Menees
The Right Reverend Dr. Ray Sutton
The Right Reverend Stephen Wood

INTRODUCTION

Two thousand years ago in Israel, the man who is God incarnate and Israel's Messiah, Jesus of Nazareth, led his followers into a life-giving relationship with himself and his divine Father, and was executed by the Roman governor. Risen from the dead, he charged his followers to make disciples throughout the whole world, promising that he would be with them, and equipping them for their mission with his Holy Spirit. Founded upon God's revelation to Israel in the Old Testament, the New Testament presents the essential witness and teaching of Jesus' first disciples, the apostles, who proclaimed his truth with his authority. The faith of Christians today, as in every age, is shaped and defined by this apostolic account of Jesus Christ.

Within a century of Jesus' earthly ministry, Christian congregations could be found throughout the Roman world, from Spain to Persia and from North Africa to Britain. By this time, the *catechumenate* for those wishing to become Christians had become established Christian practice. From the Greek *katēcheō* ("instruct"), the catechumenate was a period of one-to-three-years' instruction (*catechesis*) leading to Baptism at Easter. This ancient pattern of Christian disciple-making continued for some centuries before falling into disuse as nominal Christianity increasingly became a universal aspect of Western culture.

The Reformation era of the sixteenth century saw a vigorous renewal of catechesis for both adults and children among both Protestants and Catholics. But catechesis has been in serious decline since the eighteenth century, and much of the discipline of discipling has been abandoned altogether in today's churches.

This *catechism* (a text used for instruction of Christian disciples) is designed as a resource manual for the renewal of Anglican catechetical practice. It presents the essential building blocks of classic catechetical instruction: the Apostles' Creed, the Lord's Prayer, and the Ten Commandments (or Decalogue). To these is added an initial section especially intended for those with no prior knowledge of the Gospel. Each section is presented in the question and answer form that became standard in the sixteenth century because of its proven effectiveness. Each question and answer offers essential teaching together with biblical references for group or individual study.

In one respect, this catechism breaks new ground for Anglicans. The historic 1662 Catechism in the English Book of Common Prayer is brief and specifically designed to prepare young people for confirmation and church membership. However, this present work is intended as a more comprehensive catechetical tool for adult (or near-adult) inquirers, and for all Christians seeking deeper grounding in the full reality of Christian faith and life.

As such, this catechism attempts to be a missional means by which God may bring about both conversion to Christ and formation in Christ (or regeneration and sanctification, to use older words). This vision of comprehensive usefulness has been before the minds of the writing team from the beginning.

Our guidelines in drafting have been as follows:

1. Everything taught should be compatible with, and acceptable to, all recognized schools of Anglican thought, so that all may be able confidently to use all the material.
2. Everything taught should be expressed as briefly as possible, in terms that are clear and correspond to today's use of language. There should be as little repetition as possible, though some overlap is inevitable.

3. All the answers and questions should be as easy to explain and to remember as possible.

We offer this catechism to the Church with the prayer that it may serve to build up the Body of Christ by helping many to come to full Christian faith and faithfulness in today's increasingly post-Christian world.

On behalf of the Committee for Catechesis
of the Anglican Church in North America

The Reverend Canon J. I. Packer

CONCERNING
SCRIPTURE
REFERENCES

This catechism's Scripture references, which follow each question and answer, support its sound teaching with passages from both the Old and New Testaments. The references generally follow a lectionary-style approach, with passages drawn from the Old Testament, the Psalms, the Gospels, Acts, and the New Testament Epistles. These references are not merely "proof texts" demonstrating that an answer is scriptural. Rather, they are for deeper reflection, study, and exposition of the truth taught by the answer. In addition to the direct commands, clear principles, and explicit teachings of Scripture, they often include important stories, types, and images that reveal or point to Jesus Christ. In this way, the catechism upholds the Anglican belief that the entirety of Scripture professes Jesus Christ as Lord.

O God, who wonderfully created, and yet more wonderfully restored, the dignity of human nature: Grant that we may share the divine life of him who humbled himself to share our humanity, your Son Jesus Christ our Lord; who lives and reigns with you, in the unity of the Holy Spirit, one God, for ever and ever. **Amen.**

PART I

BEGINNING
WITH CHRIST

INTRODUCTION

This catechism is designed to teach you what it means to be a Christian. It shows you what is essential for Christian faith and life. It will open for you the door to knowing Jesus Christ and experiencing the wonder of God's love through him. If you follow its teaching, it will help you to become a citizen of God's kingdom and fully involved in the life and mission of his Church. And it will anchor you in the reality of God's unquenchable joy, beginning in this life and ever increasing in the life to come.

However, one can understand these things and still remain apart from them. In order to know God's love for you, you need to know and love Jesus Christ, and commit yourself to him as his lifelong disciple in his community, the Church. This opening section of the catechism will help you to take that step, if you have not done so already.

Whether or not you were raised in the Church, to be a Christian requires a deliberate, personal commitment to Jesus Christ, much like the commitment a person makes in marriage. Being a Christian is a process of continuing forward in faithfulness to Jesus from that point on. In order to make this commitment to Jesus, you need to know the essentials about who he is and what he has done for you. This is the Gospel ("good news") of Jesus Christ.

THE GOSPEL

God created the world and made us to be in loving relationship with him. Though created good, human nature became fatally flawed, and we are now all out of step with God. In Bible language, we are sinners, guilty before God and separated from him.

The good news of the Gospel is that God took loving action in Jesus Christ to save us from this dire situation. The key facts of this divine remedy are these: God the Father sent his eternal Son into this world to reconcile us to himself, to free us to love and serve him, and to prepare us to share his glory in the life to come. Jesus was born of the Virgin Mary through the Holy Spirit, lived a perfect life, died for our sins, and rose bodily from the dead to restore us to God. Given authority by his Father, Jesus now rules in heaven as King over all things, advancing God's kingdom throughout the world. In the fullness of time, Jesus will return to establish his kingdom in its glory on earth, and all things will be renewed.

Reigning in heaven over all things, Jesus Christ continues to draw sinners to himself. He enables us by his Holy Spirit to turn wholeheartedly from our sinful and self-centered ways (repentance), and to entrust ourselves to him to live in union and communion with him (faith). In spiritual terms, sin is the way of death, and fellowship with Christ is the way of life.

TURNING TO CHRIST

Turning to Christ brings us into fellowship with God. Baptism, which is the rite of entry into the Church's fellowship, marks the beginning of this new life in Christ. The apostle Peter, proclaiming the Gospel, said, "Repent and be baptized every one of you in the name of Jesus Christ for the forgiveness of your sins, and you will receive the gift of the Holy Spirit" *(Acts 2:38)*.

Through faith, repentance, and Baptism we are spiritually united to Jesus and become children of God the Father. Jesus said: "I am the way, and the truth, and the life. No one comes to the Father except through me" *(John 14:6)*. As we come to the Father through Jesus Christ, God the Holy Spirit enlightens our minds and hearts to know him, and we are born again spiritually to new life. To continue to live faithfully as Christians, we must rely upon the power and gifts which the Holy Spirit gives to God's people.

When the disciple Thomas encountered the risen Jesus, he acknowledged him by saying, "My Lord and my God!" *(John 20:28)*. To be a Christian you must, like Thomas, wholeheartedly submit to the living Christ as your Lord and God. Knowing the Lord Jesus means personally believing in him, surrendering your life to him through repentance and Baptism, and living as one of his joyful followers.

A clear way to make this commitment of faith and repentance is to offer to God a prayer in which you

- confess your sins to God, being as specific as possible, and repent by turning from them;
- thank God for his mercy and forgiveness given to you in Jesus Christ;
- promise to follow and obey Jesus as your Lord;
- ask the Holy Spirit to help you be faithful to Jesus as you grow into spiritual maturity.

One example of such a prayer is the following:

Almighty Father, I confess that I have sinned against you in my thoughts, words, and actions (especially _____). I am truly sorry and humbly repent. Thank you for forgiving my sins through the death of your Son, Jesus. I turn to you and give you my life. Fill and strengthen me with your Holy

Spirit to love you, to follow Jesus as my Lord in the fellowship of his Church, and to become more like him each day. **Amen.**

NEXT STEPS

To be a Christian is to be included in God's family, the Church. No one should try to be a Christian alone. If you are making this commitment for the first time—or have not been a practicing Christian for some time—here are some further steps to take:

- Share your commitment as soon as possible with one or more Christians and with an ordained minister, so they can pray for you.
- If you are not connected with a church, join a biblically faithful one. If you are connected but not involved, look for ways to deepen your participation.
- If you are now becoming a follower of Jesus Christ and have never been baptized, it is important that you speak with a minister about preparing for Baptism. It is also important to pray for God's help and spiritual protection.
- If you are a baptized Christian but have not been living out your faith, it is appropriate for you to confess your sins and reaffirm your faith in the presence of a minister.
- In order to grow in your new life in Christ, it is vitally important that you be involved in regular worship, Bible study, prayer, and Christian fellowship.

Coming to personal faith in Christ is a momentous decision that is often not made quickly. If you are not yet ready to take this step, but you continue to seek after God, you may want to pray a prayer like the following:

O God, please reveal yourself to me. Draw near to me as I seek you. Open my eyes to see your truth. Show me those things in my mind and heart that keep me from faith in you. Help me to know and trust Jesus Christ. And lead me to those people who can help me as I seek to know you.

God will always answer such prayers made with patience, persistence, and humility. As you explore this catechism, continue to pray that you will come to know God more fully.

In order to provide clarity and further detail, and for the purposes of teaching and learning, these things will now be set out in question and answer form.

SALVATION

1. What is the human condition?

Though created good and made for fellowship with our Creator, humanity has been cut off from God by self-centered rebellion against him, leading to lawless living, guilt, shame, death, and the fear of judgment. This is the state of sin. *(Genesis 3:1–13; Psalm 14:1–3; Matthew 15:10–20; Romans 1:18–23; 3:9–23)*

2. What is the Gospel?

The Gospel is the good news that God loves the world and offers salvation from sin through his Son, Jesus Christ. *(Psalm 103:1–13; Isaiah 53:4–5; John 3:16–17; 1 Corinthians 15:1–5)*

3. How does sin affect you?

Sin alienates me from God, my neighbor, God's good creation, and myself. Apart from Christ, I am hopeless, guilty, lost, helpless, and walking in the way of death. *(Genesis 3:14–19; Psalm 38; Isaiah 53:6; 59:1–2; Romans 6:20–23)*

4.　What is the way of death?

The way of death is a life without God's love and Holy Spirit, a life controlled by things that cannot bring me eternal joy, leading only to darkness, misery, and eternal condemnation. *(Genesis 2:16–17; Deuteronomy 28:15–19; Proverbs 14:12; John 8:34; Romans 1:24–25)*

5.　Can you save yourself from the way of sin and death?

No. I have no power to save myself, for sin has corrupted my conscience, confused my mind, and captured my will. Only God can save me. *(Psalm 33:13–19; Isaiah 43:8–13; John 3:1–8; Ephesians 2:1–9)*

6.　How does God save you?

God forgives my sins and reconciles me to himself through his Son, Jesus Christ, whom he has given to the world as an undeserved gift of love. "God so loved the world, that he gave his only Son, that whoever believes in him should not perish but have eternal life." *(John 3:16; see also Psalm 34; Zechariah 12:10–13:2; Romans 3:23–26)*

7.　Why does God save you?

Because he loves me, God saves me from sin and judgment, so that I may love and serve him for his glory. *(Psalm 98; Isaiah 42:5–9; John 3:17; Romans 5:8–10; 2 Corinthians 5:18–21; Ephesians 1:3–14)*

8.　Who is Jesus Christ?

Jesus is the eternal Son of God, the Savior of the world. Fully divine, he took on our human nature, died on the Cross for our sins, rose from the dead, ascended into heaven, and now rules as Lord and King over all creation. *(Numbers 21:4–9; Psalm 110; John 3:13–15; Philippians 2:5–11; Colossians 1:15–20)*

9. **Is there any other way of salvation?**

No. The apostle Peter said of Jesus, "There is salvation in no one else" *(Acts 4:12)*. Jesus is the only one who can save me and reconcile me to God. *(Psalm 2; Isaiah 42:1–4; John 14:5–6; 1 Timothy 2:5–6)*

10. **How should you respond to the Gospel of Jesus Christ?**

As soon as I receive and believe the Gospel, I should repent of my sins, put faith in Jesus Christ as my Savior and Lord, and prepare to be baptized. "Now is the day of salvation." *(2 Corinthians 6:2; see also Psalm 32; Isaiah 55:6–7; Acts 2:37–39)*

11. **What does it mean for you to repent?**

To repent means that I have a change of heart, turning from sinfully serving myself to serving God as I follow Jesus Christ. I need God's help to make this change. *(Psalm 51:16–17; Isaiah 57:15–19; Acts 3:19–21; 1 John 2:1–2)*

12. **What does it mean for you to have faith?**

To have faith means that I believe the Gospel is the truth: that Jesus died for my sins, rose from the dead, and rules over my life. Therefore, I entrust myself to him as my Savior, and I obey him as my Lord. *(Psalm 40:1–10; Proverbs 3:5–8; John 1:9–13; Romans 10:9–10; Hebrews 11:1, 6)*

13. **How can you repent and put your faith in Jesus Christ?**

With God's help, I can acknowledge and turn from my sins, receive the gift of God's grace in Jesus Christ, and embrace the new life he freely gives me. [One way to do this is by sincerely praying in the way described in the "Turning to Christ" section above, p. 20.] *(Psalm 86:1–7; Joel 2:32; Acts 16:30–34; Romans 10:11–13; Hebrews 12:1–2)*

14.   **What should you do as the sign of your repentance and faith?**
After receiving instruction in the faith, I should be baptized into the death and resurrection of Jesus Christ, thus joining his Body, the Church. If I have already been baptized, I should confess my sins, seek the guidance of a minister, affirm the promises made at my Baptism, and take my place as a member of the Church. *(Psalm 51:5–7; Ezekiel 36:25–27; Matthew 28:19–20; 1 Corinthians 12:13; 1 Peter 3:18–22)*

15.   **What does God grant in your new life in Christ?**
God grants me reconciliation with him *(2 Corinthians 5:17–19)*, forgiveness of my sins *(Colossians 1:13–14)*, union with him in Christ *(Romans 6:3–5)*, adoption into his family *(Galatians 4:4–7)*, citizenship in his kingdom *(Ephesians 2:19–21; Philippians 3:20)*, new life in the Holy Spirit *(Titus 3:4–5)*, and the promise of eternal life *(John 3:16; 1 John 5:12)*.

16.   **What does God desire to accomplish in your life in Christ?**
God desires to free me from captivity to sin and transform me into the image of Jesus Christ, by the power of his Holy Spirit. *(Exodus 33:18–23; 34:29–35; Psalm 27:4, 7–14; Matthew 17:1–9; Romans 6:5–11; 2 Corinthians 3:12–18)*

17.   **By what means will God transform you into the image of Jesus Christ?**
The first Christians "devoted themselves to the apostles' teaching and the fellowship, to the breaking of bread and the prayers" *(Acts 2:42)*. Following this pattern, I will be transformed within the life of the Church through reading Scripture and receiving the sacraments, through worship and prayer, and through fellowship with God's people and loving witness to the world. *(Deuteronomy 6:1–9; 2 Chronicles 7:1–3; Psalm 1; Acts 2:42–47; Hebrews 10:23–25)*

A Prayer for God's Love

Almighty God, you so loved the world that you gave your only Son, that whoever believes in him would not perish but have eternal life: Pour into our hearts that most excellent gift of love by your Holy Spirit, that we may delight in the inheritance that is ours as your sons and daughters, and live to your praise and glory, through Jesus Christ. **Amen.**

PART II

BELIEVING
IN CHRIST

THE APOSTLES' CREED
AND THE LIFE OF FAITH

All genuine Christians affirm that authentic Christianity is apostolic Christianity. Apostolic Christianity rests on the historic, eyewitness testimony of Jesus' first followers, the apostles, to the actual events of Jesus' life, death, resurrection, ascension, present heavenly reign, and promised future return. Both Jesus and his apostles understood these events to fulfill the Old Testament hopes of the kingdom (that is, the reign) of God. God's covenant with Israel prepared for this kingdom, which the Christian Church has received from Jesus and his apostles.

We learn from Scripture about these key events, including what they mean and how they hold together. Anglicans therefore affirm that the Holy Scriptures of the Old and New Testaments, which are contained in the Bible, are "God's Word written" *(Articles of Religion, 20)*.

By the second century, these essentials of apostolic faith had been organized into an outline of topics for instruction (the Rule of Faith), and this outline came to be known as the Apostles' Creed because it sums up the apostolic faith. This Creed came to be widely used by the Church as the declaration of faith made at Baptism and was later included as one of three creeds in the 1662 Anglican Prayer Book. The Apostles' Creed is the briefest and most easily memorized of these creeds, and is complemented and enlarged upon by the later Nicene and Athanasian Creeds.

To gather and focus the central truths of apostolic faith is the first task of all catechesis (instruction). That is precisely what the Apostles' Creed does. It is arranged in three paragraphs, which highlight in turn the work of God, the Father, the Son, and the Holy Spirit, thus distilling the teaching of Holy Scripture and reflecting the triune nature of God. It is a summary of biblical truths that is designed to lead inquirers into a grounded personal faith in the triune God.

The Apostles' Creed exists to define and defend this commitment, which is basic to being a Christian. The article on God the Creator (the Father) introduces the Creed; its central article—focused on the Person and Work of Jesus Christ—is the fullest and longest; and the article on the Holy Spirit and Christian salvation follows. As a whole, the Creed testifies to the vital core of God's self-revelation for our salvation. It is a consensus declaration that comes to us with the resounding, universal endorsement of faithful believers over nearly two thousand years. It has been recited by Christian communities throughout the history of the Church. And it is a benchmark of orthodoxy—that is, of right belief—guiding our understanding of God's revealed truth at points where our sin-clouded minds might go astray.

CONCERNING THE CREEDS

18. What is a creed?

A creed is a statement of faith. The word "creed" comes from the Latin *credo*, which means "I believe." *(Deuteronomy 11:18–23; 26:1–11; John 20:24–29; 1 John 5:9–12)*

19.   **What is the purpose of the creeds?**

The purpose of the creeds is to declare and safeguard for all generations essential truths about God, the Church, and the world, as revealed in Holy Scripture. *(Deuteronomy 7:9–11; Psalm 145:4–13; John 20:30–31; 2 Timothy 1:13–14; Hebrews 2:1–4)*

20.   **What does belief in the creeds signify?**

Belief in the creeds signifies acceptance of God's revealed truth and the intention to live by it. To reject any element of the creeds signifies a departure from the Christian faith. *(Matthew 16:13–20; 2 Timothy 3:14–15; 4:1–5; James 2:10–26)*

21.   **Which creeds has this church received?**

This church believes the Apostles' Creed, the Nicene Creed, and the Athanasian Creed. *(Articles of Religion, 8)*

22.   **Why do you receive and believe these creeds?**

I receive and believe these creeds with the Church because they are grounded in Holy Scripture and are faithful expressions of its teaching. *(Proverbs 13:14; 1 Corinthians 15:3–11; Philippians 2:5–11)*

23.   **Why should you know these creeds?**

I should know these creeds because they state the essential beliefs of the Christian faith. *(Deuteronomy 11:18–19; 1 Timothy 6:20–21; 2 Timothy 1:13–14)*

24.   **What is the Apostles' Creed?**

The Apostles' Creed says:

> I believe in God, the Father almighty,
>   creator of heaven and earth.

I believe in Jesus Christ, his only Son, our Lord.
 He was conceived by the Holy Spirit
 and born of the Virgin Mary.
 He suffered under Pontius Pilate,
 was crucified, died, and was buried.
 He descended to the dead.
 On the third day he rose again.
 He ascended into heaven,
 and is seated at the right hand of the Father.
 He will come again to judge the living and the dead.
I believe in the Holy Spirit,
 the holy catholic Church,
 the communion of saints,
 the forgiveness of sins,
 the resurrection of the body,
 and the life everlasting. **Amen.**

CONCERNING HOLY SCRIPTURE

25. What is Holy Scripture?

Holy Scripture is "God's Word written" *(Articles of Religion, 20)*, given by the Holy Spirit through prophets and apostles as the revelation of God and his acts in human history, and is therefore the Church's final authority in all matters of faith and practice. *(Psalm 19:7–11; Jeremiah 36:1–8; 2 Timothy 3:14–17; Revelation 1:1–11)*

26. What books are contained in Holy Scripture?

The thirty-nine books of the Old Testament and the twenty-seven books of the New Testament together form the whole of Holy Scripture. *(Articles of Religion, 6)*

27. What is in the Old Testament?

The Old Testament proclaims God's creation of all things; mankind's original disobedience; God's calling of Israel to be his people; his Law, wisdom, and saving deeds; and the teaching of his prophets. The Old Testament bears witness to Christ, revealing God's intention to redeem and reconcile the world through Christ. *(Luke 24:44; 1 Corinthians 10:1–4; Hebrews 11)*

28. What is in the New Testament?

The New Testament proclaims Jesus Christ's birth, life, ministry, death, resurrection, and ascension; the Church's early ministry; the teaching of the apostles; the revelation of Christ's eternal kingdom; and the promise of his return. *(Luke 24:45–49; Acts 1:1–11; Philippians 2:5–11)*

29. How are the Old and New Testaments related to each other?

The Old Testament is to be read in the light of Christ, and the New Testament is to be read in light of God's revelation to Israel. Thus the two form one Holy Scripture, which reveals the Person of Jesus Christ and his mighty works. As Saint Augustine says, "The New is in the Old concealed, the Old is in the New revealed." *(Augustine of Hippo, Questions in the Heptateuch 2.73; see also Matthew 5:17–18; Luke 24:25–27)*

30. What does it mean that Holy Scripture is inspired?

Holy Scripture is "God-breathed," for the biblical authors wrote under the guidance of God's Holy Spirit to record God's Word. *(Deuteronomy 8:3; Matthew 4:4; 2 Timothy 3:16–17; 2 Peter 1:19–21)*

31. What does it mean that Holy Scripture is the Word of God?

The Old and New Testaments are inspired by the Holy Spirit and are therefore the Word of God written. God is revealed in his mighty works and in the incarnation of our Lord, which are made known through the inspired writings of the biblical authors. God "has spoken through the prophets" *(Nicene Creed)* and continues to speak through Scripture today. *(Psalm 33:4–9; Jeremiah 1:9; Ezekiel 2:1–3:4; 1 Thessalonians 2:13; 2 Peter 3:15–16; Hebrews 1:1–2)*

32. Why is Jesus Christ called the Word of God?

The fullness of God's revelation is found in Jesus Christ, who not only fulfills the Scriptures, but is himself God's Word, the living expression of God's mind. The Scriptures testify about him, "In the beginning was the Word," and "The Word became flesh and dwelt among us" *(John 1:1, 14)*. Therefore, "ignorance of the Scriptures is ignorance of Christ." *(Jerome, Commentary on Isaiah, prologue; see also Genesis 1:26–27; Psalm 33:1–12; Colossians 1:15–19)*

33. How should Holy Scripture be understood?

Because Holy Scripture was given by God to the Church, it should always be understood in ways that are faithful to its own plain meaning, to its entire teaching, and to the Church's historic interpretation. It should be translated, read, taught, and obeyed accordingly. *(Nehemiah 8:1–8; Psalm 94:8–15; Acts 8:26–35; 18:24–28; Jerusalem Declaration, Article 2; Articles of Religion, 20)*

34. How does the Holy Spirit use Holy Scripture in your life?

Through Holy Scripture, the Holy Spirit will teach, rebuke, correct, and train me in the righteousness that God desires. The prayerful study of Scripture forms me for life in Christ and the service of God and my neighbor. *(Psalm 119:105; John 14:26; 2 Timothy 3:16–17; Hebrews 4:12–13; see questions 227–32)*

35. What are the Apocrypha?

The fourteen books of the Apocrypha, historically acknowledged by this church, are pre-Christian Jewish writings that provide background for the New Testament and are included in many editions of the Bible. They may be read as examples of faithful living but "not to establish any doctrine." *(Articles of Religion, 6)*

THE APOSTLES' CREED, ARTICLE I

"I BELIEVE IN GOD"

36. Who is God?

God is one divine Being eternally existing in three divine Persons: the Father, the Son, and the Holy Spirit. This is the Holy Trinity. *(Deuteronomy 6:4–7; Psalm 86:8–10; Isaiah 44:6–8; Matthew 3:16–17; 28:19; 1 Corinthians 8:6; 2 Corinthians 13:14)*

37. What does Holy Scripture tell us about the character of God?

God is both loving and holy. God mercifully redeems fallen creation, while righteously opposing all sin and evil. The Lord Jesus Christ is the fullest revelation of God's holy love. *(Exodus 34:6–7; Psalm 145; John 1:14–18; 14:9–10; Romans 5:6–11; Hebrews 1:1–3)*

"THE FATHER ALMIGHTY"

38. Who is God the Father?

God the Father is the first Person of the Holy Trinity, from whom the Son is eternally begotten and the Holy Spirit eternally proceeds. *(Psalm 104; John 1:1, 14; 15:26; 1 Corinthians 2:10–16; 1 Peter 1:10–12; Nicene Creed)*

39.   Why do you call the first of the three divine Persons "Father"?
Our Lord Jesus Christ is the only divine Son of the Father. He called God "Father" and taught his disciples to do the same. God gives believers his Holy Spirit and adopts us as his children, enabling us to call him "Father." *(Deuteronomy 32:4–9; Psalm 2; Matthew 6:6–9; John 5:17–23; Galatians 4:1–7)*

40.   What do you mean when you call God "Father"?
When I call God "Father," I declare that I was created for relationship with him, that I trust in God as my Protector and Provider, and that I put my hope in God as his child and heir in Christ. *(Genesis 1:26–27; Psalms 68:4–6; 103:13–14; Matthew 6:25–34; Romans 8:17–21)*

41.   Why do you call God the Father "Almighty"?
I call the Father "Almighty" because he has power over everything and accomplishes everything he wills. Together with his Son and Holy Spirit, the Father is all-knowing and ever present in every place. *(Psalm 139:1–16; Isaiah 40:12–26; Daniel 4:34b–37; Luke 1:34–37; Revelation 4:8b–11)*

"CREATOR OF HEAVEN AND EARTH"

42.   Why do you call God the Father "Creator"?
I call God the Father "Creator" because he made all things. He creates and sustains all things through his Word, and gives life to all creatures through his Spirit. *(Genesis 1:1–2:3, 7; Psalm 104:24–30; John 1:1–3; Acts 17:24–28; Colossians 1:16–18)*

43.   How does recognizing God as Creator inform your understanding of his creation?
I acknowledge that God created for his own glory everything that exists. He created human beings, male and female, in his image

and appointed us stewards of creation. God's creation is thus a gift to enjoy as we work and care for it. *(Genesis 1:27–28; 2:15; Psalm 8:5–8; Luke 19:11–27; 1 Corinthians 4:1–2)*

44. What does it mean that God created both heaven and earth?
It means that all things, whether visible or invisible, physical or spiritual, were brought into being out of nothing by the Word of the eternal God. *(Genesis 1:1–8; Psalm 33:6–8; John 1:3; Colossians 1:16)*

45. Was the world that God created good?
Yes. God created all things and called them "very good" *(Genesis 1:31)*. However, through sin, evil and death have come into the world and corrupted it. *(Genesis 3:1–8; Psalm 14:1–3; Matthew 15:18–20a; Romans 1:18–32; 1 Timothy 4:4–5)*

46. If God created the world good, why do we sin?
Adam and Eve rebelled against God, thus bringing upon all humanity pain, toil, alienation from God and each other, and death. I have inherited this fallen and corrupted human nature; consequently, I too sin and fall short of God's glory. *(Genesis 3:16–4:26; Psalm 51:3–5; Romans 3:23; 5:12; 7:14–25)*

47. What are the consequences of sin?
Because of sin, those apart from Christ are spiritually dead, separated from God, under his righteous condemnation, and without hope. *(Genesis 3:16–19; Psalm 90:3–12; Isaiah 53:6; John 3:36; Romans 6:20–23; Galatians 5:19–21; Ephesians 2:1–3)*

A Prayer for the Father's Love

Gracious Father, I come to you through the saving work of your Son Jesus Christ upon the Cross. Thank you for adopting me as your child through the Holy Spirit. Grant me the grace to know the fullness of your fatherly love, that I may delight in the promises of your eternal Kingdom, both now and in the age to come. **Amen.**

THE APOSTLES' CREED, ARTICLE II

"I BELIEVE IN JESUS CHRIST"

48. Who is Jesus Christ?

Jesus Christ is the eternal Word and Son of God, the second Person of the Holy Trinity. He took on human nature to be the Savior and Redeemer of the world, the only Mediator between God and fallen humanity. *(Psalm 2; Malachi 3:1; John 1:1–18; Philippians 2:5–11; 1 Timothy 2:5–6)*

49. What does "Jesus" mean?

"Jesus" means "God saves" and is taken from the Hebrew name *Yeshua* or Joshua. In Jesus, God has come to save us from the power of sin and death. *(Joshua 1:1–9; Psalm 20; Matthew 1:18–25; Romans 8:1–2)*

50. What does "Christ" mean?

Christos is the Greek term for the Hebrew title *Messiah*, meaning "Anointed One." Old Testament kings, priests, and prophets were anointed with oil. Jesus the Christ was anointed by the Holy Spirit to perfectly fulfill these roles, and he rules now as Prophet, Priest, and King over his Church and all creation. *(Exodus 40:12–16; 1 Samuel 16:11–13; 1 Kings 19:15–16; Psalm 89:19–29; Luke 3:21–22; 4:14–21; Acts 10:38; Hebrews 4:14–5:10)*

"HIS ONLY SON, OUR LORD"

51. Why is Jesus called the Father's "only Son"?

Jesus alone is God the Son, coequal and coeternal with God the Father and God the Holy Spirit. He alone is the image of the invisible Father, the one who makes the Father known. He is now and forever will be incarnate as a human, bearing his God-given human Name. The Father created and now rules all things in heaven and earth through Jesus Christ our Lord. *(Psalm 2:7–12; John 1:14–18; Colossians 1:13–15; Hebrews 1:1–5; see also Athanasian Creed)*

52. What do you mean when you call Jesus Christ "Lord"?

I acknowledge Jesus' divine authority over the Church and all creation, over all societies and their leaders, and over every aspect of my life, both public and private. I surrender my entire life to him and seek to live in a way that pleases him. *(Daniel 7:13–14; Matthew 7:21–23; Luke 9:23–26; Ephesians 1:15–23; Colossians 1:16–18)*

"HE WAS CONCEIVED BY THE HOLY SPIRIT AND BORN OF THE VIRGIN MARY"

53. What does it mean that Jesus was conceived by the Holy Spirit?

Jesus was conceived not through a human father but by the Holy Spirit coming upon the Virgin Mary in power. *(Isaiah 7:14; Matthew 1:18–20; Luke 1:26–38)*

54. What happened at Jesus' conception in Mary's womb?

The eternal Son, whom God named Jesus, assumed a fully human nature from his mother, the Virgin Mary, at the moment of conception in her womb. *(John 1:1–3, 14; 8:56–58; Philippians 2:6–8; Colossians 2:9)*

55. **Why is it important to say that Jesus was born?**

It is important to affirm that he is one of us: truly human, born to a human mother, and raised in a human family. *(Luke 2:41–52; Hebrews 2:17–18)*

56. **Was Mary the only biological parent of Jesus?**

Yes. While still a virgin, Mary submitted to the will of God and bore the Son of God. Therefore, she is held in high honor. However, in obedience to God, Joseph took Mary as his wife and raised Jesus as his son. *(Isaiah 7:14; Matthew 1:18–25; 13:55)*

57. **What is the relationship between Jesus' divine and human natures?**

At the moment of Jesus' conception, the divine nature of the one eternal Person of the Son was united to our human nature. Therefore, Jesus Christ is fully and truly both divine and human, but without sin. His two natures are united without division, separation, mixture, or change. *(Luke 1:26–38; John 1:14; Philippians 2:6–8; Hebrews 2:10–16; 1 John 4:2–3; Definition of Chalcedon)*

58. **What does the union of Jesus' two natures teach you about his ministry?**

All Jesus does as a human being he also does as God. His human words and deeds are saving because they are the words and deeds of God the Son. *(John 5:19–29; Romans 8:1–4; Colossians 1:19–23; Hebrews 4:14–16)*

"HE SUFFERED UNDER PONTIUS PILATE"

59. **Why did Jesus suffer?**

Jesus suffered as a sacrifice for our sins so that we could have peace with God, as prophesied in the Old Testament: "But he was pierced for our transgressions; he was crushed for our iniquities; upon him was the chastisement that brought us peace, and with his wounds we are healed." *(Isaiah 52:13–53:12, see 53:5; John 1:29; Romans 6:23; 1 Corinthians 15:3–4)*

60. In what ways did Jesus suffer?

On earth, the incarnate Son shared physically, emotionally, and spiritually in the temptations and sufferings common to all people, yet without sin. In his agony and desolation on the Cross, he uniquely suffered in my place for my sins and, in so doing, revealed God's love and compassion for fallen and suffering humanity. *(Psalm 22:1–24; Matthew 4:1–10; 27:26–50; Hebrews 4:14–16)*

61. How do Jesus' sufferings help you?

Jesus has experienced our sufferings, understands our sorrows, and is able to sympathize with our weakness. Therefore, I should bear my sufferings with perseverance and hope, for my Savior is with me in them, and through them I will come to know him more fully. *(Job 9:32–35; Psalm 22:22–26; Isaiah 53:4–7; Luke 4:1–13; Hebrews 4:14–5:10)*

62. Why does the Creed say that Jesus suffered under the Roman governor Pontius Pilate?

The Creed thus makes clear that Jesus' life and death were real events that occurred at a particular time and place in Judea in the first century AD. *(Psalm 2:1–6; Luke 3:1–2; 23; Acts 4:24–28).*

"WAS CRUCIFIED, DIED, AND WAS BURIED" "HE DESCENDED TO THE DEAD"

63. What happened at Jesus' crucifixion?

Jesus was executed as a common criminal. He was scourged, mocked, and nailed to a Cross outside the walls of Jerusalem. Though humanly a miscarriage of justice, his execution fulfilled God's plan of salvation. *(Psalm 22:1–21; Isaiah 53:8; Matthew 27:22–26)*

64. What did Jesus accomplish on the Cross?

Jesus fulfilled the Scriptures by dying on the Cross as a sacrifice for sin in obedience to his Father. He thereby showed the depth of the love of God for his fallen creation, satisfying the justice of God on our behalf and breaking the power of sin, Satan, and death. *(Leviticus 23:18–21; Psalm 34:15–22; Colossians 2:13–15; Hebrews 10:11–14)*

65. What does Jesus' death mean for you?

Jesus bore my sins and died the death that I deserve, so that I could be saved from sin and eternal condemnation and reconciled to God. *(Psalm 32:1–2; Isaiah 53:10–12; Matthew 20:28; Romans 5:8–10; 2 Corinthians 5:17–21)*

66. Why does the Creed make a point of saying that Jesus died?

The Creed makes the point to emphasize that Jesus died a real, bodily death such as all people face because of our sins. *(Psalm 22:14–15; Isaiah 53:8–9; Matthew 27:45–50; John 19:30–35)*

67. Why does the Creed emphasize Jesus' death in this way?

The Creed emphasizes Jesus' death to counter suspicions that Jesus did not truly die on the Cross, to celebrate the fact that he died there to secure our salvation, and to prepare our minds to grasp the glory of his bodily resurrection. *(John 19:31–34; 1 John 5:6–8)*

68. What does the Creed mean by saying that Jesus descended to the dead?

That Jesus descended to the dead means that he truly died and entered the place of the departed. *(Psalm 16:9–10; Acts 2:25–32; Ephesians 4:9–10; 1 Peter 3:18–19)*

"ON THE THIRD DAY HE ROSE AGAIN"

69. What does the Creed mean when it affirms that Jesus rose again from the dead?

It means that Jesus was not simply resuscitated; God restored him physically from death to life in his resurrected body, never to die again. His tomb was empty; Jesus had risen bodily from the dead. The risen Jesus was seen by his apostles and hundreds of other witnesses. *(Psalm 30:1–5; Luke 24:1–12; John 20:1–18; Acts 1:3; 1 Corinthians 15:3–8)*

70. What kind of earthly life did Jesus have after he rose from the dead?

Following his resurrection, Jesus spent forty days visiting and teaching his followers. He appeared to his disciples, spoke to them, invited them to touch him and see his scars, and ate with them. *(Luke 24:13–49; John 20:19–29; Acts 1:1–8)*

"HE ASCENDED INTO HEAVEN"

71. How should you understand Jesus' ascension into heaven?

Jesus was taken up out of human sight and returned in his humanity to the glory he had shared with the Father before his incarnation. There he intercedes for, and receives into heavenly life, all who come to him in faith. Though absent in body, Jesus is always with me by his Spirit and hears me when I pray. *(John 17:5; Acts 1:9–11; Romans 8:34; Hebrews 7:23–25)*

72. What resulted from the ascension?

Jesus ascended into heaven so that, through him, his Father might send us the gift of the Holy Spirit. Through the Holy Spirit, Christians together are united to Christ, the living Head of his Body, the Church. *(John 14:15–17, 25–26; 16:7–15; Acts 2:33–36; Ephesians 4:7–16)*

"AND IS SEATED AT THE RIGHT HAND OF THE FATHER"

73. What does it mean for Jesus to sit at God the Father's right hand?

The throne on the king's right hand was traditionally the seat of one appointed to exercise the king's own authority. Ruling with his Father in heaven, Jesus is Lord over the Church and all creation, with authority to equip his Church, advance his kingdom, bring sinners into saving fellowship with God the Father, and finally establish justice and peace upon the earth. *(Psalm 2; Isaiah 9:6–7; Acts 2:33–36; Ephesians 1:20–23; Hebrews 1:3–14)*

74. What does Jesus do for you as he sits at the Father's right hand?

Because Jesus intercedes for us as our great high priest, I may now boldly approach the Father and offer my confessions, praises, thanksgivings, and requests to him. *(Exodus 33:7–17; Psalm 80; Hebrews 4:14–16; 7:24–8:2)*

75. What does Jesus' heavenly ministry mean for your life today?

I can rely on Jesus always to be present with me by the Holy Spirit as he promised, and I should always look to him for help as I seek to serve him. *(Joshua 1:9; Psalm 3; Matthew 28:20; John 14:15–20)*

"HE WILL COME AGAIN TO JUDGE THE LIVING AND THE DEAD"

76. What does the Creed mean when it says, "He will come again"?

Jesus promised that he would return *(Luke 21:27–28)*. His coming in victory with great glory and power will be seen by all people and will bring this age to an end. The present world order will pass away, and God will usher in a fully renewed creation to stand forever. All the saints will be together with God at that time. *(Proverbs 30:4; Daniel 7:13–14; Luke 21:27–28; Acts 1:10–11; 1 Thessalonians 4:13–18; 2 Peter 3:3–13; Revelation 21:1–4)*

77. Can we know when Jesus will return?

No. We cannot know when Jesus will return. Jesus patiently waits for many to repent and trust in him for new life; then he will return unexpectedly, which could be at any moment. *(Matthew 24:36–44; 1 Thessalonians 5:1–3)*

78. How should you live in anticipation of Jesus' return?

I should anticipate with joy the return of Jesus my Savior and be ready to stand before him. His promise to return encourages me to be filled with the Holy Spirit, to live a holy life, and to share the hope of new life in Christ with others. *(Deuteronomy 30:1–10; Matthew 25:13–30; 1 Thessalonians 5:4–11; Titus 2:11–14)*

79. How should you understand Jesus' future judgment?

All people, whether living or dead, will be judged by Jesus Christ. Those apart from Christ will receive eternal rejection and punishment in hell, while those who are in Christ will receive eternal blessing and welcome into the fullness of life with God. *(Psalm 50:1–6; Matthew 25:31–46; Romans 2:16; 2 Corinthians 5:10)*

80. Should you be afraid of God's judgment?

The unrepentant should fear God's judgment, for "the wrath of God is revealed from heaven against all ungodliness" *(Romans 1:18)*. But if I am in Christ, I need not fear God's judgment, for my Judge is my Savior, Jesus Christ, who loves me, died for my sins, and intercedes for me. *(Psalm 130; Proverbs 28:13–14; John 5:24–30; Romans 8:1, 31–34)*

81.   **What does Scripture mean when it tells you to fear God?**

It means that I should live mindful of his presence, walking in humility as his creature, resisting sin, obeying his commandments, and reverencing him for his holiness, majesty, and power. *(Exodus 20:18–20; Psalm 25:12–14; Proverbs 9:10; Acts 5:1–11; 1 Peter 1:13–21; Revelation 14:6–7)*

82.   **How do you rightly live in the fear of God?**

With the help of the Holy Spirit, I examine my conscience according to the Word of God. Particularly useful are the Ten Commandments and the Sermon on the Mount, as well as the godly counsel of fellow Christians and the moral teaching of the Church. *(Exodus 20:1–17; Psalm 139:23–24; Matthew 5–7; 1 Corinthians 4:1–5)*

83.   **How does the Church exercise its authority to judge?**

The authority Christ gave to his Church to judge is most often exercised by declaring God's forgiveness in absolution. However, a priest, acting under the authority of the bishop, may suspend a person from receiving Communion because of scandalous and unrepented sin, in order to draw them to repentance and restoration. *(Psalm 32; Matthew 16:19; 18:15–17; John 20:21–23; 1 Corinthians 5:1–13)*

A Prayer for the Son's Mission

O Jesus, God the Son, in your incarnation you manifested your heart of mission in the world: Help me so to know and practice your presence, that I may always live for your glory and the spread of your Kingdom; who with the Father and the Holy Spirit, lives and reigns, one God, now and forever. **Amen.**

THE APOSTLES' CREED, ARTICLE III

"I BELIEVE IN THE HOLY SPIRIT"

84. Who is the Holy Spirit?

God the Holy Spirit is the third Person in the one Being of the Holy Trinity, coequal and coeternal with God the Father and God the Son, and equally worthy of our honor and worship. *(Genesis 1:2; Psalm 104:30; Matthew 3:16–17; 28:19; John 15:26; 2 Corinthians 13:14)*

85. What principal names does the New Testament give to the Holy Spirit?

Jesus names the Holy Spirit "Paraclete" ("the one alongside"), which signifies Comforter, Guide, Counselor, Advocate, and Helper. Other descriptions for the Holy Spirit are "Spirit of God," "Spirit of your Father," "Spirit of Christ," and "Spirit of truth." *(Matthew 10:20; John 14:16–17, 26; Acts 16:7; Romans 8:9)*

86. What are the particular ministries of the Holy Spirit?

The Holy Spirit imparts life to every living thing in creation, reveals God's Word to his people, and calls sinners to a new life of faith in the saving and life-giving work of Jesus. The Holy Spirit unites Christians to Jesus, indwelling them, convicting them of sin, giving them spiritual gifts, and bearing spiritual fruit in their lives. *(1 Samuel 16:13; Psalm 143:7–12; Isaiah 11:2; Joel 2:28–29; John 15:26; 16:7–11; Acts 4:5–31)*

87. How does the Holy Spirit strengthen you for life in Christ?

The Holy Spirit bears witness that I am a child of God, stirs my heart continually to worship and to pray, and inspires me to holiness and good works in Christ. *(Job 27:2–4; Matthew 10:19–20; John 14:12; 16:12–15; Acts 6:10; 13:2; Romans 8:15–17, 26–27)*

88. How do you receive the Holy Spirit?

The Scriptures teach that, by repenting and being baptized in the Name of Jesus Christ, I am forgiven my sins and I receive the Holy Spirit, who gives me new birth in Christ and frees me from the power of sin. *(Luke 11:11–13; John 3:1–7; Acts 2:38; 8:14–17; 19:1–6; 1 Corinthians 6:9–11; 12:13; 2 Timothy 1:6–7)*

89. What is the fruit of the Holy Spirit?

The fruit of the Holy Spirit is the very character of Jesus developing in us through the work of the Holy Spirit: "love, joy, peace, patience, kindness, goodness, faithfulness, gentleness, self-control." *(Galatians 5:22–25; see also Matthew 7:15–20; 12:33–35)*

90. What are the gifts of the Holy Spirit?

Among the many gifts of the Holy Spirit named in the New Testament are faith, healing, miracles, prophecy, discernment of spirits, other languages ("tongues"), the interpretation of other languages, and words of wisdom and knowledge. The Spirit distributes gifts to individuals as he wills for the sake of the Body of Christ. Other gifts in the New Testament include administration, service, encouragement, evangelism, teaching, giving, leadership, and mercy. Jesus promises that the Father will give the Holy Spirit to those who ask. *(Luke 11:13; Romans 12:3–8; 1 Corinthians 12:7–31; Ephesians 4:7–11; 1 Peter 4:10–11)*

91. Why does the Holy Spirit give such gifts?

The Holy Spirit equips and empowers believers with gifts for service in the worship of Jesus Christ, for the building up of his

Church, and for witness and mission to the world. *(Exodus 31:1–11; Luke 9:1–6; 1 Corinthians 12:12–26; Ephesians 4:12–16)*

A Prayer for the Holy Spirit's Ministry

Come, Holy Spirit, fill the hearts of your faithful people and kindle in me the fire of your love. Direct and rule my heart in all things, empower me for witness and ministry, and daily increase in me your gifts and fruit, to the glory of God the Father; through Jesus Christ our Lord. **Amen.**

"THE HOLY CATHOLIC CHURCH"

92. What is the Church?

The Church is the whole community of faithful Christians in heaven and on earth, called and formed by God into one people. The Church on earth gathers to worship God in Word and Sacrament, to serve God and neighbor, and to proclaim the Gospel to the ends of the earth. *(Exodus 19:4–6; Psalm 22:22–23; Matthew 28:19–20; Ephesians 2:11–22; 1 Peter 2:4–10; Articles of Religion, 19)*

93. How does Holy Scripture teach you to view the Church?

Holy Scripture teaches me to view the Church as God's family, as the Body and bride of Christ, and as the temple where God in Christ dwells by his Spirit. *(Isaiah 54:5–8; Hosea 2:16–20; Matthew 12:46–50; 1 Corinthians 3:16–17; 2 Corinthians 6:14–7:1; Revelation 5:9–10; 19:6–10)*

94. Why is the Church called the Body of Christ?

The Church is called the Body of Christ because all who belong to the Church are united to Christ as their Head and source of life, and are united to one another in Christ for mutual love and service to him. *(Romans 12:4–5; 1 Corinthians 12:12–27; Ephesians 1:22–23; 5:25–30)*

95. What are the "marks" or characteristics of the Church?

The Nicene Creed expands upon the Apostles' Creed to list four characteristics of the Church: it is "one, holy, catholic, and apostolic." *(see Articles of Religion, 8)*

96. In what sense is the Church "one"?

The Church is one because all its members form the one Body of Christ, having "one Lord, one faith, one baptism, one God and Father of all" *(Ephesians 4:5–6)*. The Church is called to embody this unity in all relationships between believers. *(Psalm 133; John 17:11, 20–23; Ephesians 2:11–22; 4:2–6)*

97. Why is the Church called "holy"?

The Church is holy because the Holy Spirit dwells in it and sanctifies its members, setting them apart to God in Christ and calling them to moral and spiritual holiness of life. *(Exodus 19:3–6; Leviticus 19:1–2; 20:22–26; Psalm 15; John 17:17–19; Acts 26:16–18; 1 Corinthians 3:16–17; Colossians 3:12–15)*

98. Why is the Church called "catholic"?

The Church is called "catholic" ("according to the whole") because it keeps the whole faith it has received from the Lord, in continuity with the whole Church, in all times and places. *(Micah 4:1–4; Acts 2:1–11; 1 Corinthians 15:1–8; 2 Timothy 1:13–14; Jude 3; Revelation 5:9–10)*

99. Why is the Church called "apostolic"?

An apostle is one who is sent. The Church is called "apostolic" because it holds the faith of the first apostles sent by Christ. In continuity with them, the Church is likewise sent by Christ to proclaim the Gospel and to make disciples throughout the whole world. *(Matthew 10:1–4, 40–42; 28:18–20; Acts 2:42; 13:1–4; Ephesians 2:19–21)*

"THE COMMUNION OF SAINTS"

100. Who are the saints?

The saints are all those in heaven and on earth who place their faith in Jesus Christ, who are set apart, holy to God in Christ, and transformed by his grace. *(Leviticus 19:1–2; Deuteronomy 7:6; Psalm 16:1–3; 1 Peter 2:4–10; Revelation 7:9–17)*

101. What does the word "communion" mean?

"Communion" means being "one with" someone in union and unity. For Christians, it refers to the unity of the three Persons within the one Being of God, to our union with God through our union with Christ, and to our unity with one another in Christ. *(Psalm 85; Ezekiel 37:24–28; John 17:20–26; 2 Corinthians 13:11–14; 1 John 1:1–3)*

102. What is the "communion of the saints"?

The communion of the saints is the fellowship of all those, in heaven and on earth, who are united in Christ as one Body, through one Spirit, in Holy Baptism. *(Psalm 149; Ephesians 2:13–22; Hebrews 12:1–3)*

103. How do you participate in the communion of the saints?

I live as a member of the communion of saints through faith in Jesus Christ and the work of the Holy Spirit by gathering to worship God with my fellow Christians, by praying for and encouraging one another, and by coming to one another's aid in times of trouble, sickness, or grief. *(Psalm 133; Acts 2:42–47; Colossians 3:16; 1 Thessalonians 5:11–18; Hebrews 10:24–25; James 5:13–20)*

104. How are the Church on earth and the Church in heaven joined in worship?

Through union with Christ, as celebrated in the sacrament of Holy Communion, the Church on earth participates with the Church in heaven in the eternal worship of God. *(Exodus 24:9–11; Psalm 148; 1 Corinthians 10:16–17; Hebrews 12:18–29; Revelation 19:1–9)*

"THE FORGIVENESS OF SINS"

105. What are sins?

Sins are intentions, acts, or failures to act that arise out of my corrupted human nature and fall short of conformity to God's revealed will. *(Psalm 53; Isaiah 59:1–15; Jeremiah 17:9; Romans 3:23; James 4:17; 1 John 3:4–10)*

106. How does God respond to human sin?

All sin is opposed to the righteousness of God and is therefore subject to God's holy condemnation; yet God in his mercy offers me forgiveness and salvation from sin through his Son, Jesus Christ, the only Savior. *(Psalm 130; Isaiah 1:2–4; Micah 7:18–19; John 3:17–21; Romans 1:18–2:4; 3:24–26; 5:6–10)*

107. How does God forgive your sins?

By virtue of Christ's atoning sacrifice, in which I put my trust, God sets aside my sins, accepts me, and adopts me as his child and heir in Jesus Christ. Loving me as his child, he forgives my sins whenever I turn to him in repentance and faith. *(Leviticus 26:40–45; Psalm 78:35–39; Matthew 26:27–28; Luke 15:11–32; 2 Corinthians 5:16–21; Galatians 4:1–7)*

108. How should you respond to God's forgiveness?

Trusting in God's continual forgiveness, I should live in continual thanks, praise, and obedience to him; and as I have been loved and forgiven by God, so I should love and forgive those who sin against me. *(Psalm 51:7–17; Isaiah 44:21–23; Matthew 6:12; 18:21–35; Ephesians 4:32)*

109. What is grace?

Grace is God's undeserved gift of his love, mercy, and help, which he freely offers to us who, because of our sin, deserve only condemnation. *(Genesis 50:15–21; Psalm 106; Joel 2:12–13; Luke 7:36–50; Romans 5:15–21; Ephesians 2:4–9; Hebrews 4:14–16)*

110. For what purpose does God give you grace?

God gives me grace in Christ for the forgiveness of my sins, redemption from sin's power, healing of sin's effects, and growth in holiness, to my final transformation into the likeness of Christ. *(Psalms 25:6–12; 119:29–32; Jonah 3; Matthew 9:1–8; Romans 6:1–11; 2 Corinthians 3:16–18; Titus 3:4–7)*

111. Can you earn God's grace?

No. God gives his grace freely and enables me to receive it. Everything I do for God should be in response to his love and grace made known in Christ, for "while we were still sinners, Christ died for us," and "we love because he first loved us." *(Romans 5:8; 1 John 4:19; see also Exodus 34:5–10; Psalm 23; John 10:7–18; Ephesians 2:1–10; 2 Timothy 1:8–10)*

112. Is God's grace only for your religious or spiritual life?

No. God wants to redeem every aspect of my life, and his grace in Christ is at work in all of it. *(Psalm 40; Isaiah 1:13–20; Matthew 6:25–33; Titus 2:11–14)*

113. Does God give grace only to Christians?

No. God's common grace can be seen in his provision for all people. "He makes his sun rise on the evil and on the good, and sends rain on the just and on the unjust" *(Matthew 5:45)*. However, he shows his saving grace by granting salvation to those who place their faith in Christ. *(Psalms 65:5–13; 145:8–9; Acts 14:15–17; Romans 5:1–11)*

"THE RESURRECTION OF THE BODY"

114. What does Holy Scripture tell you about your body?

Holy Scripture tells me that my body, though tainted by sin, was created good, bearing the image of God and endowed with great dignity. Therefore, from the moment of conception to natural death, every human body and every human life should be cared for, protected, and loved. *(Genesis 1:26–28; Psalm 139:7–18; Matthew 11:2–5; 1 Corinthians 6:19–20; James 3:8–10)*

115. Why will you die?

Because sin and death now corrupt this world, my body will degenerate and die. But, by the will of God, my soul will be with the Lord, and I will rise bodily from death when Jesus Christ returns to judge the living and the dead. *(Genesis 2:15–17; 3:22–24; Psalm 82:7; Ecclesiastes 2:16; John 6:35–40; Romans 5:12–14; 1 Corinthians 15:13–28)*

116. What is the resurrection of the body?

When the risen Lord Jesus returns to judge the earth, he will raise all the dead to bodily life. The wicked will then receive eternal condemnation, and the righteous eternal life in the glory of God. *(Psalm 16; Ezekiel 37:1–14; Daniel 12:1–3; Matthew 25:31–34, 41, 46; John 5:25–29; 1 Thessalonians 4:13–17; Revelation 20:11–15)*

117. What do you know about the resurrected bodies of believers?

They will be fully renewed and glorified in the image of Christ, perfected after the manner of his own resurrected and ascended body. *(Job 19:25–27; John 11:23–27; 1 Corinthians 15:35–58; Philippians 3:20–21)*

118. **How should you live as you await the resurrection of your body?**

Because I put my hope in God's resurrection of my body, I should honor and care for it. I should refrain from any violence, disrespect, or sin that would harm, demean, or violate either my body or the bodies of others. *(Psalm 35:9–10; Matthew 25:35–45; Romans 6:5–14; 1 Corinthians 6:9–20; 1 John 3:1–3)*

"AND THE LIFE EVERLASTING"

119. **What do you know about the unending resurrected life of believers?**

I know that it will be an eternal life of joyful fellowship with our triune God, together with all his saints and angels, singing his praises and serving him in the renewed creation. *(John 17:20–24; Revelation 7:9–17; 21:1–4; 21:22–22:5)*

120. **How should you live in light of this promise of unending life?**

I should live in joyful expectation of the fullness of my transformation, soul and body, into the likeness of Christ. In the midst of suffering or in the face of hostility and persecution, I am sustained by the hope of a new heaven and earth, freed from Satan, evil, suffering, and death. *(Psalm 21:1–7; John 14:1–7; Romans 13:11–14; 2 Corinthians 4:16–5:11; Philippians 3:7–21; 1 Peter 1:3–9; 5:6–11)*

CONCERNING SACRAMENTS

121. **What is a sacrament?**

A sacrament is an outward and visible sign of an inward and spiritual grace. God gives us the sign as a means by which we receive that grace and as a tangible assurance that we do in fact receive it. *(Genesis 17:1–21; John 6:53–58; Romans 2:25–29; 1 Corinthians 10:16; 1662 Catechism)*

122. How should you receive the sacraments?

I should receive the sacraments by faith in Christ, with repentance and thanksgiving. Faith in Christ is necessary to receive the grace of the sacraments, and obedience to Christ is necessary for the benefits of the sacraments to bear fruit in my life. *(Mark 16:16; John 6:52–58; Acts 2:38–47; 1 Corinthians 11:27–32; 1662 Catechism; Articles of Religion, 28)*

123. What sacraments were ordained by Christ?

The two sacraments ordained by Christ that are "generally necessary to salvation" *(1662 Catechism)* are Baptism and Holy Communion (also called the Lord's Supper or the Holy Eucharist). These are sometimes called "sacraments of the Gospel." *(Articles of Religion, 25; see also Matthew 28:19–20; Luke 22:14–20; John 6:52–58; 1 Corinthians 11:23–26; 2 Corinthians 1:21–22)*

124. Are there other sacraments?

Other rites and institutions commonly called sacraments include confirmation *(2 Timothy 1:6–7; Hebrews 6:1–2)*, ordination *(Numbers 8:9–14; 27:18–23; 1 Timothy 4:14)*, marriage *(Genesis 2:18–24; Matthew 19:4–6; John 2:1–11)*, absolution *(John 20:21–23; Acts 2:37–41)*, and the anointing of the sick *(James 5:14)*. These are sometimes called "sacraments of the Church."

125. How do these differ from the sacraments of the Gospel?

They were not ordained by Christ as necessary to salvation, but arose from the practices of the apostles and the Early Church, or were blessed by God in Scripture. God clearly uses them as means of grace. *(Articles of Religion, 25)*

126. What is the outward and visible sign in Baptism?

The outward and visible sign is water, in which candidates are baptized "in the Name of the Father, and of the Son, and of the Holy Spirit." *(Book of Common Prayer 2019; see also Genesis 9:8–17; Matthew 28:19–20; 1 Peter 3:18–22)*

127. What is the inward and spiritual grace given in Baptism?

The inward and spiritual grace is death to sin and new birth to righteousness, through union with Christ in his death and resurrection. I am born a sinner by nature, separated from God. But in Baptism, through faith in Christ and the gift of the Holy Spirit, I am made a member of Christ's Body and adopted as God's child and heir. *(Psalm 51:1–2, 7–10; Ezekiel 36:25–26; John 3:3–5; Romans 6:1–11; Colossians 2:9–14)*

128. What is required of you when you come to be baptized?

Two things are required: repentance, in which I turn away from sin; and faith, in which I turn to Jesus Christ as my Savior and Lord and trust the promises that God makes to me in this sacrament. *(Psalm 51:3–6, 13–17; Mark 1:14–15; Acts 2:37–38)*

129. Why is it appropriate to baptize infants?

Because it is a sign of God's promise that they are embraced in the covenant community of Christ's Church. Those who in faith and repentance present infants to be baptized vow to raise them in the knowledge and fear of the Lord, with the expectation that they will one day profess full Christian faith as their own. *(Deuteronomy 6:6–9; Proverbs 22:6; Mark 2:3–5; Acts 2:39; 16:25–34)*

130. **What signs of the Holy Spirit's work should you hope and pray to see as a result of your Baptism?**

I should hope and pray that the Holy Spirit, who indwells me, will help me to be an active member of my Christian community, participate in worship, continually repent and return to God, proclaim the faith, love and serve God and my neighbor, and seek justice and peace. *(Matthew 22:35–40; Hebrews 10:19–28; 12:14; 1 Peter 3:15; 1 John 1:9; 2:1)*

HOLY COMMUNION

131. **Why did Christ institute the sacrament of Holy Communion?**

He instituted it for the continual remembrance of the sacrifice of his atoning death, and to convey the benefits of that sacrifice to us. *(Exodus 24:1–10; Psalm 23:5–6; Luke 22:17–20; John 6:25–51; 1 Corinthians 10:16–17)*

132. **What is the outward and visible sign in Holy Communion?**

The visible sign is bread and wine, which Christ commands us to receive. *(1 Corinthians 11:23–26)*

133. **What is the inward gift signified?**

The inward gift signified is the Body and Blood of Christ, which are truly taken and received in the Lord's Supper by faith. *(Deuteronomy 8:1–20; Psalm 78:17–29; John 6:52–56; 1 Corinthians 10:1–4, 16–18)*

134. **What benefits do you receive through partaking of this sacrament?**

As my body is nourished by the bread and wine, my soul is strengthened by the Body and Blood of Christ. I receive God's forgiveness, and I am renewed in the love and unity of the Body of Christ, the Church. *(1662 Catechism; Psalms 28:6–9; 104:14–15; Jeremiah 31:31–34; John 6:52–56; 17:22–24; Revelation 19:6–9)*

135. **What is required of you when you come to receive Holy Communion?**

I am to examine myself: Do I truly repent of my sins and intend to lead a new life in Christ? Do I have a living faith in God's mercy through Christ and remember his atoning death with a thankful heart? And have I shown love and forgiveness to all people? *(Leviticus 10:1–5; Psalm 50; 1 Corinthians 11:27–32)*

136. **What is expected of you after partaking in Holy Communion?**

I should continue to grow in holiness, avoiding sin, showing love and forgiveness to all, and serving others in gratitude. *(Leviticus 20:26; 1 Corinthians 10:14–32; 1 Peter 4:1–11)*

CONFIRMATION

137. **What is confirmation?**

Confirmation is the laying on of the bishop's hands with prayer for strengthening by the Holy Spirit, following a period of catechetical formation. In confirmation, I make a mature confession of faith, publicly renewing the vows and promises made at my Baptism. *(Deuteronomy 6:4–25; Psalm 119:33–40; Acts 8:14–17; 2 Timothy 1:6–7)*

138. **What grace does God give you in confirmation?**

In confirmation, I am further empowered and gifted by the Holy Spirit for daily growth in wisdom, courage, and humility before God in every aspect of my life and work. *(Psalms 37:3–31; 71:17–18; Isaiah 11:2–5; Acts 19:6; Jude 3, 17–25; "Confirmation, Reception, and Reaffirmation," Book of Common Prayer 2019)*

139. **What is the work of all Christians?**

All Christians are to bear witness to Christ in their lives; to care for the poor, strangers, widows, and orphans; and, according to their gifts, to serve Christ in the world and in the Church. *(Zechariah 7:9–10; Psalms 1; 15; Micah 6:6–8; Colossians 3:1–17; James 1:27; 1 Peter 4:8–11)*

ORDINATION

140. **What is ordination?**

Ordination is the laying on of the bishop's hands with prayer, which confirms the gifts and calling of the candidates, consecrates them, and grants them authority to serve Christ and his Church in the office to which they have been called. *(Isaiah 6:1–8; Luke 9:1; Acts 6:1–7; 13:1–3; 1 Timothy 3:1–13; 4:14; 5:22; Titus 1:5–9)*

141. **What grace does God give in ordination?**

In ordination, God conveys the gift of the Holy Spirit for the office and work of the order being conferred. *(Numbers 27:12–23; Ephesians 4:7–16; 2 Timothy 1:6–7)*

142. **What are the three ordained ministries in the Anglican Church?**

The three orders are bishops, priests, and deacons, which we have received from Scripture and the historic Church. *(Acts 6:1–7; 1 Timothy 3:1; 5:17–22; 2 Timothy 4:5; Titus 1:5; Ignatius of Antioch, Letter to the Trallians 2.1–3; 3.1–2)*

143. **What is the work of bishops?**

Bishops represent and serve Christ and the Church as chief pastors, catechists, and missionaries in the tradition of the apostles. They are to confirm and ordain, and to guard the faith, unity, and discipline of the Church. *(Isaiah 61:1–11; John 20:19–23; 21:15–19; Acts 20:17–35; 1 Timothy 3:1–7; Titus 1:7–9; 1 Peter 5:1–5; Ignatius of Antioch, Letter to Polycarp 1.2–2.2)*

144. What is the work of priests?

Serving Christ with their bishops, priests (or presbyters) nurture God's people through the ministry of Word and Sacrament and pronounce absolution and blessing in God's Name. *(Genesis 14:17–20; Psalm 132:8–18; Luke 10:1–9; John 10:1–16; Ephesians 4:7–13)*

145. What is the work of deacons?

Serving Christ under their bishops, deacons care for those in need, assist in public worship, and instruct both young and old in the catechism. *(Deuteronomy 15:7–11; Psalm 119:1–8; Luke 12:35–40; Acts 6:1–7; 1 Timothy 3:8–13)*

MARRIAGE

146. What is Christian marriage?

Christian marriage, or Holy Matrimony, is a lifelong covenant between one man and one woman, uniting them in self-giving love, joy, and faithfulness. It is ordained by God for the procreation and spiritual nurture of children, the sanctification of husband and wife, the mutual support of their common life, and the flourishing of family, church, and society. Husband and wife enter into this covenant by exchanging vows before God and in the presence of witnesses. *(Genesis 2:18–25; Song of Solomon 4:7–10; Matthew 19:3–9; John 2:1–11; Romans 7:2–3; Hebrews 13:4; see questions 322–23)*

147. What is signified in marriage?

The union of husband and wife in one flesh signifies the communion between Christ, the heavenly bridegroom, and the Church, his holy bride. Not all are called or able to marry, but all Christians are joined to Christ as members of his Body. *(Song of Solomon 8:6–7; Isaiah 54:4–8; 1 Corinthians 7:6–11; Ephesians 5:22–33; Revelation 19:6–10; 21:1–4)*

148. What grace does God give in marriage?

In Christian marriage, God unites husband and wife and blesses their common life, that they may grow together in love, wisdom, and godliness, patterned on the sacrificial love of Christ. A Christian marriage embodies this grace in the world, especially through hospitality and care for those who are lonely or in need. *(Genesis 2:18–25; Psalm 128; Proverbs 18:22; Matthew 1:18–25; 1 Corinthians 13:1–13; "Holy Matrimony," Book of Common Prayer 2019)*

ABSOLUTION

149. What is absolution?

In absolution, a priest, acting under God's authority, pronounces God's forgiveness in response to repentance and confession of sin. *(2 Samuel 12:1–13; Proverbs 28:13; John 20:22–23; James 5:15–16)*

150. What grace does God give to you in absolution?

In absolution, God conveys his pardon through the Cross, removes and cancels my sin, declares me reconciled and at peace with him, and grants me the assurance of his grace and salvation. *(Psalm 32; Matthew 18:18; Acts 5:30–32; 1 John 1:8–10)*

151. What is necessary to receive the grace of absolution?

Repentance, in which I intend to resist further sin, accept responsibility for my actions, and endeavor to repair damage I have caused; and faith, by which I thankfully receive God's forgiveness. *(1 Kings 8:46–53; Psalm 51; Daniel 9:1–23; Matthew 3:1–12; Romans 2:1–11; 2 Corinthians 7:5–13)*

ANOINTING OF THE SICK

152. What is the anointing of the sick?

Through prayer and anointing with oil, the minister invokes God's blessing upon those suffering in body, mind, or spirit. *(1 Kings 17:17–24; Psalm 107:17–22; Matthew 8:14–17; 10:5–8; Acts 28:8; James 5:15–16)*

153. What grace does God give in the anointing of the sick?

God gives healing, strength, and peace, either for recovery from injury or illness, or for perseverance in adversity, especially in preparation for death. *(Psalms 103:2–5; 119:49–56; Isaiah 49:13; Matthew 8:5–13; 2 Corinthians 1:3–7; 12:7–10)*

A Historic Prayer for the Church

> O God of unchangeable power and eternal light: Look favorably on your whole Church, that wonderful and sacred mystery; by the effectual working of your providence, carry out in tranquility the plan of salvation; let the whole world see and know that things which were cast down are being raised up, and things which had grown old are being made new, and that all things are being brought to their perfection by him through whom all things were made, your Son Jesus Christ our Lord; who lives and reigns with you, in the unity of the Holy Spirit, one God, for ever and ever. **Amen.** *(Fifth Century Collect, Book of Common Prayer 2019)*

PART III

BELONGING
TO CHRIST

THE LORD'S PRAYER AND
THE CHRISTIAN LIFE

The Gospel is God's invitation to know him, to love and serve him as members of his family, and to be transformed into his likeness. God continually calls his people to grow deeper in our relationship with him. Thus, for Christians, knowing and loving God is life's central activity, and a primary way we do this is through prayer. Prayer is the way God has given us to listen and respond to him.

The most important prayer in the Christian faith is the Lord's Prayer, so named because it is the prayer the Lord Jesus himself, the Son of the Father, taught his disciples to pray *(Matthew 6:9–13; Luke 11:2–4)*. It is vital for our lives as present-day disciples. It teaches us to know God as our Father, to submit our wills to his will, and to live in this world as citizens of God's kingdom, even as we await with hope the fullness of its coming. For this reason, it has been included as a prayer in both public and private Christian worship from the very beginning of the Church's life.

However, the Lord's Prayer is also a pattern by which we shape all our prayers. It teaches us different kinds of prayer, and a mature life of prayer will include them all: praise of God's glory, intercession for the needs of others, petition for our needs and protection, and confession of our sin. While the Lord's Prayer does not include all types of prayer, it establishes a central core of prayers for our entire life in Christ. It teaches us *how* to pray and is therefore an essential aspect of Christian catechesis.

Our primary resource for prayer as Anglicans, in addition to the Scriptures, is the Book of Common Prayer. The Lord's Prayer has a central place in Prayer Book worship and is included in every service. However, beyond providing us forms of prayer, the Book of Common Prayer also gives us a *rule of prayer*—a way of ordering our lives around a daily pattern of prayer and the reading of Scripture. A well-rounded rule will include the different kinds of prayer mentioned above, in both public worship and private devotion. While the form of rule may vary from person to person, the purpose of every rule is to help us grow in prayer. As our capacity to pray increases, so our daily habits of prayer broaden to encompass the whole scope of our lives. And, little by little, we begin to understand what Saint Paul means to "pray without ceasing" *(1 Thessalonians 5:17)*, for that is the goal of our life of prayer in Christ.

A Prayer for Spiritual Direction and Protection

Heavenly Father, you made us for yourself, and our hearts are restless until they rest in you: Direct our heartfelt desires and defend us against our Enemy, that we may pray according to your will; through Jesus Christ our Lord; who lives and reigns with you and the Holy Spirit, world without end. **Amen.**

CONCERNING PRAYER

154. **What is prayer?**

Prayer is turning my heart toward God, to listen and to speak with him. *(Psalms 84; 123; Matthew 7:7–11; John 17:1–9)*

155. What should you seek in prayer?

In prayer, I should seek not only God's provision for my needs, but fellowship with God, who made me for fellowship with himself. *(Exodus 33:7–11; Psalms 27:4, 8; 42:1–2; John 14:18–23; 1 John 1:3)*

156. How can you have fellowship with God?

Through the death and resurrection of Jesus, and union with him by the Holy Spirit, I have fellowship with God as his adopted child. I experience this in prayer, worship, God's Word, the sacraments, and Christian community, as I daily follow him by faith. *(Nehemiah 9:1–8; Psalm 65:1–4; John 15:9–17; Acts 2:42–47; Romans 8:14–17; 1 John 1:3–7)*

157. Why should you pray?

I should pray because God calls me to do so, because I was made for fellowship with him, because I need the help of his Holy Spirit, and because he has promised to answer the prayers of his people. *(Exodus 33:7–11; Psalm 50:14–15; Matthew 7:7–11; Luke 18:1–8; Romans 8:26; 1 Timothy 2:1)*

158. What should you pray?

I should pray the Lord's Prayer, the Psalms, the collected prayers of the Church, and my own prayers as the Spirit leads me. *(1 Samuel 2:1–10; Psalms 2; 62:8; Luke 1:46–55; 2:25–35; Acts 4:24–30; Romans 8:26–27; Revelation 4:8–11)*

159. When should you pray?

I should pray at regular times throughout each day, with fellow Christians for prayer and worship, and whenever I am aware of a need for God's grace. And I should learn to "pray without ceasing" *(1 Thessalonians 5:17)* as I grow in the knowledge of God's presence. *(Nehemiah 2:4; Psalm 55:17; Daniel 6:10; Jonah 2; Matthew 15:21–28; 1 Thessalonians 5:16–18; Hebrews 4:16; 5:7)*

THE LORD'S PRAYER

160. **What is the prayer our Lord Jesus taught his disciples to pray?**

The traditional version of the Lord's Prayer is this:

Our Father, who art in heaven,
    hallowed be thy Name,
    thy kingdom come,
    thy will be done,
    on earth as it is in heaven.
Give us this day our daily bread.
And forgive us our trespasses,
    as we forgive those
    who trespass against us.
And lead us not into temptation,
    but deliver us from evil.
For thine is the kingdom,
    and the power, and the glory,
    for ever and ever. **Amen.**
    (Matthew 6:9–13; see also Luke 11:2–4)

161. **Why should you learn the Lord's Prayer?**

I should learn the Lord's Prayer because Jesus taught it to his disciples as both a practice and a pattern for prayer to God the Father. *(Matthew 6:5–8; Luke 11:1, 5–13)*

162. **Why should you practice the Lord's Prayer?**

I should pray the Lord's Prayer regularly because it teaches me to pray as Jesus commanded and to desire what his Father wills. *(Psalm 34; Matthew 12:46–50; 26:36–44; 1 John 5:14–15)*

163. **How is the Lord's Prayer a pattern for prayer?**
The Lord's Prayer models the primary types of prayer: praise of God, intercession for his rule, petition for his provision and protection, and confession of sins. I should pray regularly in all these ways. *(Psalm 150; Isaiah 63:7–64:12; Acts 9:36–43; 3 John 2)*

164. **What are the parts of the Lord's Prayer?**
The traditional form of the Lord's Prayer begins by addressing God the Father, makes seven petitions, adds a doxology, and concludes with "Amen."

THE ADDRESS: "OUR FATHER, WHO ART IN HEAVEN"

165. **Why do we call God "Father"?**
We call God "Father" because Jesus teaches his disciples that we are God's children and should call God "our Father." *(Exodus 4:22; Psalm 73:15; Isaiah 43:6; Matthew 23:8–9; 2 Corinthians 6:18; see questions 39–40)*

166. **Who are God's children?**
All who come to God through faith and Baptism in Christ are adopted as children of God the Father. *(Deuteronomy 32:1–6; Isaiah 30:1; John 1:12–13; Romans 8:14–16; 1 John 3:1–3)*

167. **Why does Jesus teach us to pray "our" Father?**
Jesus teaches us always to understand ourselves not only as individuals but as members of God's family of believers, and to pray accordingly. *(Psalm 147; Romans 8:14–19; 1 Peter 1:17)*

168. **How is God like earthly fathers?**
Like all loving and sincere earthly fathers, God loves us in our weakness, provides for our needs, teaches us in our ignorance,

and corrects us when we go astray. *(Psalm 103:12–14; Luke 11:11–13; Hebrews 12:5–10)*

169. How is God unlike earthly fathers?

Unlike our natural fathers, our heavenly Father loves us perfectly, is almighty in his care, makes no errors in judgment, and disciplines us only for our good. *(1 Samuel 2:12–17, 22–36; Psalm 145:8–21; Luke 11:11–13; 15:11–32; Hebrews 12:9–11)*

170. What is heaven?

Heaven is the realm of God's presence, power, and glory, which exists invisibly alongside this visible realm, and from which God hears the prayers of his children. *(1 Kings 8:27–30; Psalm 11:4; Isaiah 66:1; Matthew 18:10; John 3:31; Ephesians 4:10; Hebrews 9:24; Revelation 21:1–2)*

171. How does your Father in heaven help you here on earth?

Because God is in all places and knows all things, he hears and answers my prayers, directs my paths, and strengthens me in times of trouble. *(2 Samuel 22; Psalms 23; 46; Matthew 6:6–8, 25–34; 7:9–11; James 1:5)*

THE FIRST PETITION: "HALLOWED BE THY NAME"

172. What is the first petition?

The first petition is "Hallowed be thy Name." *(Matthew 6:9; see also Psalms 99:3; 105:1–3; John 12:27–28; see questions 283–89)*

173. What is God's Name?

God's Name reveals who he is—his nature, his character, his power, and his purposes. The Name God reveals to Moses is "I AM WHO I AM" or simply "I AM" *(Exodus 3:6, 14)*. This Name means that he alone is truly God, he is the source of his own Being, he is holy and just, and he cannot be defined by his creatures. *(Exodus 3:6, 14; 15:11; Psalm 99; Isaiah 5:16; 42:8; 47:4; John 8:58; Revelation 1:8)*

174. What are some other names for God given in Scripture?
Throughout the Scriptures, God is known as "Lord." Through the Person and ministry of Jesus Christ, God is also revealed to be one God in three Persons: the Father, the Son, and the Holy Spirit. *(Matthew 28:19; Mark 1:24)*

175. What does "hallowed" mean?
"Hallowed" means to be treated as holy—set apart, sacred, and glorified. *(Exodus 13:1–12; Leviticus 22:31–33; Deuteronomy 6:7–8; Psalm 11:4–7; Isaiah 6:1–8; Luke 2:22–35; 2 Timothy 2:19–22)*

176. How does God hallow his Name?
God's Name is holy in itself, and God glorifies his Name by saving fallen humanity, by building his Church, and by establishing his kingdom in this world and in the age to come. *(Nehemiah 9:9–10; Psalm 111:9; Ezekiel 36:22–32; Luke 1:49; John 12:23–28; Acts 4:24–31; Ephesians 5:25–27; 1 Peter 2:4–9)*

177. How can you hallow God's Name?
I can honor God's Name as holy by worshiping him, serving others, and living in loving obedience as his child and a citizen of his kingdom. *(Deuteronomy 4:6–8; Psalm 105:1–6; Ezekiel 36:16–32; Matthew 5:16; Hebrews 13:15–16)*

THE SECOND PETITION: "THY KINGDOM COME"

178. What is the second petition?
The second petition is "Thy kingdom come." *(Matthew 6:10)*

179. **What is God's kingdom?**

The kingdom of God is the just and peaceful reign of Jesus Christ over all the world, especially in the lives of his faithful people, through the powerful work of the Holy Spirit. *(Psalms 103:19; 145:11–13; Isaiah 11:1–9; Daniel 4:28–37; Mark 1:14–15; Luke 17:20–21; Ephesians 1:3–14; Colossians 1:9–14)*

180. **When you pray for God's kingdom to come, what are you asking?**

I pray that the whole creation may be renewed and restored under its rightful Lord, now in part and fully in the age to come. *(Psalm 72; Daniel 7:27; Mark 14:25; Romans 8:19–25; Philippians 2:9–11; Revelation 11:15–18; 21:5)*

181. **How does God's kingdom come?**

God's kingdom is announced to the people of Israel, arrives in Jesus Christ, and advances through the Church's mission. It will appear in its fullness once Christ returns in glory. *(Psalm 102:12–22; Daniel 2:31–45; Matthew 10:5–8; Mark 4:26–32; Acts 1:1–11; 1 Corinthians 15:19–28)*

182. **How do you live in God's kingdom?**

As a citizen of God's kingdom, I am called to live in obedience to God's Word and will, in loving witness and service to others, and in joyful hope of Christ's return. *(Psalm 15; Ezekiel 37:20–28; Mark 4:1–25; Romans 14:17; Philippians 3:17–21; 1 Peter 2:9–12)*

THE THIRD PETITION: "THY WILL BE DONE, ON EARTH AS IT IS IN HEAVEN"

183. **What is the third petition?**

The third petition is "Thy will be done, on earth as it is in heaven." *(Matthew 6:10)*

184. What is God's will?

God's will is to reconcile all things to himself in Jesus Christ and to establish his kingdom on the earth. His will is revealed in the whole of Scripture and especially in Jesus Christ, whom I am called to serve and imitate with my whole life. *(Deuteronomy 6:4–5; Psalm 119:1–16, 104–5; Proverbs 4:1–9; Matthew 22:36–40; John 6:39–40; Romans 8:28–30; 12:1–2; 2 Corinthians 5:18–19)*

185. What do you pray for as you seek God's will?

I pray for God to break the dominion of the world, the flesh, and the devil; to establish justice and thwart the plans of the wicked; to strengthen and direct his Church; and to extend the kingdom of his grace. *(Psalm 10:17–18; Matthew 16:17–18; Luke 18:7–8; Ephesians 6:10–20; 2 Thessalonians 3:1–2; 1 Timothy 2:1–4)*

186. How can you do God's will?

I can walk in God's will by loving him and my neighbor, and by taking my part in the Church's mission to extend his kingdom in the world. *(Deuteronomy 30:11–16; Psalm 15; Micah 6:8; Matthew 28:19–20; Mark 12:28–34; 1 Thessalonians 4:1–8; 1 John 2:15–17)*

187. Why do you pray, "on earth as it is in heaven"?

In heaven, God's Name is perfectly hallowed, and his will is perfectly obeyed and fulfilled. I pray for his kingdom to be established fully and his will to be accomplished on earth, that his Name may be perfectly hallowed in all creation. *(Psalm 103:19–22; Isaiah 11:1–9; Daniel 4:34–35; Ephesians 1:15–23; Revelation 4:8–11)*

THE FOURTH PETITION:
"GIVE US THIS DAY OUR DAILY BREAD"

188. What is the fourth petition?

The fourth petition is "Give us this day our daily bread." *(Matthew 6:11; see also Luke 11:3)*

189. Having prayed first for God's glory, kingdom, and will, what do you now pray?

I pray for my needs and those of my brothers and sisters: for daily provision, pardon for sins, and protection from evil. *(Psalms 25:16–18; 34:8–10; 71; Lamentations 2:19; Matthew 7:7–11; Philippians 4:6)*

190. What does "our daily bread" mean?

Daily bread includes all that we need each day for our bodily provision and spiritual nourishment. *(Exodus 16:4; Psalm 105:39–42; Proverbs 30:7–9; John 6:1–14, 41–51; Philippians 4:19)*

191. Why should you pray for daily bread?

God calls me to trust him for the needs of each day, to be concerned for the needs of others, to be content with what I have, and to grow in gratitude for his provision. *(Exodus 16; Psalm 78:15–20; Matthew 6:25–34; James 4:2–3)*

192. Why does God give you daily bread?

God gives me daily bread because he is a good and loving Father, who gives good things to all his children, sustains us in life, and desires that we grow daily in his grace. *(Psalms 103:13–14; 104:27–30; Isaiah 40:11, 29–31; Matthew 7:9–11)*

THE FIFTH PETITION:
"AND FORGIVE US OUR TRESPASSES"

193. What is the fifth petition?

The fifth petition is "Forgive us our trespasses, as we forgive those who trespass against us." *(Matthew 6:12; see also Luke 11:4)*

194. What are trespasses?

A "trespass" is a sin—a thought, word, or deed which offends God's holy character and violates his Law, missing the mark of his will and expectations. *(Isaiah 53:6; 1 John 3:4)*

195. Do you sin against God's Law?

Yes. I, together with all humankind, sin daily against God's Law, in thought, word, and deed, both by what I do and by what I fail to do. *(Psalm 14:2–3; Proverbs 20:9; Ecclesiastes 7:20; Romans 3:9–18, 23; 1 John 1:8–10)*

196. What is God's forgiveness?

God's forgiveness is his merciful pardon of sin and removal of the guilt that results from our disobedience. *(Psalms 32:1–2; 51:1–17; Isaiah 1:18; 55:6–9; Jeremiah 33:7–9; Matthew 18:23–27; Colossians 2:13–14)*

197. On what basis do you ask forgiveness?

I ask God our loving Father to forgive me through his Son, Jesus Christ, who bore my sins upon the Cross, so that through faith and Baptism I can receive his righteousness. *(Isaiah 53:4–12; Daniel 9:16–19; Luke 18:9–14; Acts 2:38; 13:38–39; Romans 5:17; Hebrews 9:11–26)*

198. Does God forgive your sins?

Yes. In Christ, God freely forgives the sins of all, including me, who sincerely repent and in true faith turn to him. *(Leviticus 16:29–34; Psalm 103:8–14; Isaiah 55:6–9; Jeremiah 31:31–34; Matthew 6:14–15; Hebrews 10:11–18; 1 John 1:9–10)*

"AS WE FORGIVE THOSE WHO TRESPASS AGAINST US"

199. Why should you forgive others?

I should forgive others because, while I was still a sinner, God forgave me through Jesus Christ. Failing to forgive impedes God's work in my life and gives opportunity to the evil one. *(Genesis 50:15–21; Psalm 133; Matthew 18:21–35; Luke 23:34; Ephesians 4:30–32; Colossians 3:12–13)*

200. How do you forgive others?

Forgiveness is a decision of my will and an attitude of my heart that seeks the good of my neighbor, and chooses not to hold against them the damage they have inflicted. I forgive whether they have asked for forgiveness or not. *(Exodus 23:4; Leviticus 19:17–18; Matthew 5:38–48; Luke 17:3–4; 23:34; Acts 7:60; Romans 12:14, 17–21; James 5:9; 1 Peter 3:9)*

201. Will your forgiveness of others always result in reconciliation?

No. Though my decision and desire to forgive may not result in my neighbor's repentance or our reconciliation, I am still called to forgive. *(Matthew 18:15–35; Romans 12:17–21)*

THE SIXTH PETITION: "AND LEAD US NOT INTO TEMPTATION"

202. What is the sixth petition?

The sixth petition is "And lead us not into temptation." *(Matthew 6:13; Luke 11:4)*

203. **What is temptation?**

Temptation is any enticement to turn from faith in God and to violate his commandments. *(Proverbs 1:8–19; James 1:14–15)*

204. **What are the sources of temptation?**

I am tempted by the false promises of the world, the selfish desires of my flesh, and the lies of the devil, all of which war against God and my spiritual well-being. *(Genesis 3:1–8; Proverbs 30:7–9; Mark 7:15; James 1:13; 1 John 2:15–17)*

205. **What help do you seek from God in the face of temptation?**

I ask God to increase my faith to trust him, enliven my conscience to fear him, soften my heart to love him, and strengthen my will to obey him, that I may resist evil and stand in the face of temptation. *(Proverbs 2; Matthew 4:11; Luke 22:31–32; 1 Corinthians 10:12–14; James 4:5–10)*

206. **Does God lead you into temptation?**

No. God never tempts anyone, nor is he the cause of any sin; but he does allow me to be tested so that I may grow in faith and obedience. *(Genesis 22:1–18; Job 1:6–12; Psalm 11:4–5; Proverbs 17:3; Matthew 4:1; James 1:12–15)*

207. **What are ways to guard against temptation?**

As I abide in Christ, I can guard against temptation by praying for protection and strength, confessing my sins, recalling God's Word, avoiding tempting situations, and seeking the support of fellow Christians. *(Genesis 39:7–12; Psalm 119:9–11; Matthew 4:1–11; Mark 14:38; Romans 13:11–14; Ephesians 6:13–18; 1 Peter 4:1–2, 7)*

208. How can the Church help you to resist temptation?

In the fellowship of Christ's Body, I can find companionship when I am lonely or vulnerable, support to resist ungodly influence, wisdom to guard me from folly, exhortation to grow in holiness, and discipline to correct me when I fall into error. *(Matthew 18:15–20; Galatians 6:1–5; 1 Thessalonians 5:11, 14–16; James 5:16)*

THE SEVENTH PETITION: "BUT DELIVER US FROM EVIL"

209. What is the seventh petition?

The seventh petition is "But deliver us from evil." *(Matthew 6:13)*

210. What is evil?

Evil is the willful perversion of God's will. Evil defies God's holiness, violates his Law, enslaves us to sin, and mars his good creation. *(Genesis 3:1–19; 4:1–8; 6:5; Proverb 1:10–19; Isaiah 59:4–13; Mark 7:20–23; 1 John 3:4)*

211. If God is good, why does he permit evil?

God created rational creatures free to love, obey, and worship him, but we have used our freedom to reject his love, rebel against him, and choose evil. Yet no evil can thwart God's purposes, and he is able to use evil to bring about even greater good. *(Genesis 6:5; Judges 2:19–23; Psalm 10; Ecclesiastes 7:29; Romans 8:18–28; Hebrews 2:8–18; Revelation 2:18–29)*

212. Is God responsible for evil?

No. The sinful choices of his creatures do not implicate God in evil in any way. *(Deuteronomy 30:15–19; Romans 7:7–25; James 1:13–15)*

213. Did evil exist before the human race embraced it?

Yes. Satan had already opposed God and chosen evil when he tempted Adam and Eve. *(Genesis 3: 1–5; John 8:44)*

214. What are Satan and his demons?

Demons, of whom Satan is chief, are fallen angels. Satan rebelled against God and led other angels to follow him. They now cause spiritual and sometimes physical harm to mortals, and they sow lies that lead to confusion, despair, sin, and death. *(Job 1–2; Daniel 10:20–21; Luke 8:26–29; 9:37–43; 11:14–26; Acts 16:16–18; 2 Thessalonians 2:9–10)*

215. How did Satan and his angels turn to evil?

Satan and his angels were overcome by envy and pride and rebelled against God. *(Isaiah 14:12–15; Ezekiel 28:12–19; 1 Timothy 3:6; Jude 6; Revelation 12:7–12)*

216. What are angels?

Angels are rational, spiritual beings created by God. God's holy angels joyfully serve him in heavenly worship, and God appoints them to act as messengers, bringing words of guidance and assurance to the faithful, and assisting and protecting them. *(Numbers 22:21–31; Psalm 148:1–6; Isaiah 6:2–3; Luke 1:19, 26–33; Acts 12:7–11; Hebrews 1:7–14; 13:2)*

217. How does God overcome evil in this world?

God has triumphed over all the powers of evil through the death, resurrection, and ascension of his Son, Jesus Christ. God will finally destroy all evil, including death, at the end of the age. *(Psalms 46; 110:1; Isaiah 52:7–10; Daniel 7:9–14; Luke 21:25–28; 1 Corinthians 15:24–28; Colossians 2:13–15; Hebrews 2:7–9, 14–15; Revelation 21:1–8)*

218. How does God redeem evil?

Though disaster, disease, death, and the evil deeds of his creatures may cause great harm and suffering, the almighty and all-wise God can use them to bring about his good purposes, both in the world and in my life. *(Genesis 50:20; Romans 5:3–5; 8:28; Hebrews 12:3–11)*

219. From what evil do you seek to be delivered?

I seek to be delivered from my own fallen inclination toward evil. I also seek God's deliverance from the devil; from the dangers of the day and night; from sorrow, sickness, and horror; from injustice and oppression; and from everlasting damnation. *(Psalm 91; Luke 18:1–8; 22:31–32; Romans 7:15–25; 2 Corinthians 1:8–11; 2 Thessalonians 3:1–2; 1 Peter 5:8–9; "The Great Litany," Book of Common Prayer 1662)*

220. How does God deliver you from evil?

Jesus has conquered the dominion of darkness and now grants me victory over sin and evil through the Holy Spirit. He transforms my mind and heart to see and oppose evil, and gives me the power to overcome it. He gives me strength to endure my trials gracefully and may even remove them from me. *(Psalm 23; Ezekiel 36:24–27; Matthew 10:16–20; John 17:11–17; 2 Corinthians 12:7–10; James 4:7–8; 1 Peter 5:8–9)*

THE DOXOLOGY AND AMEN

221. What is the doxology of the Lord's Prayer?

The doxology often added to the Lord's Prayer is "For thine is the kingdom, and the power, and the glory, for ever and ever. Amen" *(Matthew 6:13)*. A doxology is a short phrase or hymn giving glory to God. *(Ephesians 3:20–21; 1 Timothy 1:17)*

222. What does "kingdom, power, and glory" mean?

Mirroring the first half of the Lord's Prayer, the Church rejoices that God is already reigning over all creation, working out his holy will, and hallowing his Name in earth and heaven. *(1 Chronicles 29:11–13; Revelation 5:11–14)*

223. Why do you end the Lord's Prayer by saying "Amen"?

By saying "Amen," which means "so be it," I declare my agreement with the prayer. I unite with the faithful, and together we pray as Jesus commanded, believing that our petitions please the Father, and trusting that he will hear and answer us. *(Nehemiah 8:1–3, 5–6; Psalms 72:18–19; 106:48; 2 Corinthians 1:19–20; Revelation 19:1–4)*

A RULE OF PRAYER: SCRIPTURE, PRAYER, AND WORSHIP

224. What is a "rule" of prayer?

A rule of prayer is a regular discipline by which I cultivate a life of prayer and grow to love and glorify God more fully. *(Psalms 5:1–3; 119:164; Daniel 6:6–13; Mark 1:35–39; Luke 5:12–16; Ephesians 6:10–20)*

225. What can hinder your regular prayers?

My prayers may be hindered by many things, such as lethargy or loss, selfishness or sin, distractions or difficulties, or seasons of spiritual dryness. With God's help, a rule of prayer strengthens me to overcome all these. *(1 Kings 19:1–18; Psalm 116; Matthew 26:36–46; Luke 20:45–47; Romans 8:22–27)*

226. What nurtures a fruitful life of prayer?

My life of prayer is fed by the regular reading of Scripture, practice of personal prayer, and corporate worship of God. The ancient threefold rule of the Church encourages weekly Communion, the Daily Office, and private devotions to shape this way of life. *(Psalm 1; John 15:1–17; Ephesians 5:15–20; Philippians 4:8–9; Hebrews 10:19–25)*

SCRIPTURE

227. How should the Holy Scriptures shape your daily life?

I should "hear them, read, mark, learn, and inwardly digest them" that by the sustaining power of God's Word, I may grow in grace and hold fast to the hope given to me in Jesus Christ. *(Collect for the Second Sunday of Advent, Book of Common Prayer 2019; see also Deuteronomy 6:4–9; Psalm 119:1–48; Luke 2:39–52; James 1:18–27; 2 Peter 3:18)*

228. How should you "hear" the Bible?

I should hear the Bible through regular participation in the Church's worship, in which I join in reciting Scripture, hear it read and prayed, and listen to its truth proclaimed. *(Nehemiah 8:1–8, 18; Psalm 81; Luke 4:16–30; 1 Timothy 4:6–16; Revelation 1:1–3)*

229. How should you "read" the Bible?

I should read the Bible daily, following the Church's set readings (lectionaries) or following a pattern of my own choosing. *(Deuteronomy 17:18–20; Psalm 119:97–112; Acts 8:26–40)*

230. How should you "mark" passages of Scripture?

I should study the Bible attentively, noting key verses and themes, as well as connections between passages in the Old and New Testaments. I should study on my own and with other Christians, using trustworthy commentaries and other resources to grasp the full meaning of God's Word. *(Psalm 119:129–44; Luke 24:44–49; Acts 17:1–15)*

231. How should you "learn" the Bible?

I should seek to know the whole sweep of Scripture and to memorize key passages for my own spiritual growth and for sharing with others. *(Psalm 119:9–16; 2 Timothy 2:15; 3:10–17)*

232. How should you "inwardly digest" Scripture?

I should meditate on Scripture and let it shape my thoughts and prayers. As I absorb Scripture, it deepens my knowledge of God, becomes the lens through which I understand my life and the world around me, and guides my attitudes and actions. *(Joshua 1:1–9; Psalms 1:2; 119:1–8, 113–28; John 15:1–11; Colossians 3:16–17)*

PRAYER

233. Are there different ways to pray?

Yes. Prayer can be private or public, liturgical or extemporaneous, spoken or silent. *(1 Samuel 1:1–20; 1 Kings 8:22–61; Psalm 142; Matthew 11:25–28; Mark 1:35–39; Luke 6:12–16; Hebrews 5:7–10)*

234. What types of prayer are in the Lord's Prayer?

The Lord's Prayer includes praise, petition, intercession, and confession to God. *(Matthew 6:9–13; Luke 11:2–4)*

235. What is praise?

In praise, I glorify and adore God for his holiness, his sovereign rule over all, and his salvation given in Jesus Christ. *(Exodus 15:1–21; Psalm 111; Luke 1:39–56; Ephesians 1:3–14)*

236. What is petition?

In petition, I make requests to God on my own behalf for his provision and protection. *(1 Samuel 1; 2 Kings 20:1–7; Psalm 86; John 17:1–5; 2 Corinthians 12:1–10; Philippians 4:6–7)*

237. What is intercession?

In intercession, I make requests to God on behalf of others, the Church, and the world. *(Exodus 32:1–14; Psalm 20; John 17:6–26; Ephesians 3:14–21; 6:18–20)*

238. What is confession?

In confession, I acknowledge my sins in repentance before God and receive his forgiveness. *(Nehemiah 1:4–11; Psalm 51; Jeremiah 36:1–3; Luke 23:39–43; Acts 2:14–41; 2 Corinthians 7:2–12; 1 John 1:9)*

239. What types of prayer are not included in the Lord's Prayer?

Other types of prayer are thanksgiving, by which I give thanks to God for his providential goodness and answers to my prayers; and oblation, by which I offer to him all that I am and all that I do. *(2 Samuel 22; Psalm 63; Luke 1:38; 22:39–44; Romans 12:1; Hebrews 10:1–25; 13:15–16)*

240. With what attitude should you pray?

I should pray with humility, love, and a ready openness to hear and do God's will. *(2 Chronicles 7:13–15; Psalms 31; 46:10–11; Luke 18:9–14; Philippians 4:4–7)*

241. What prayers should you learn as a part of your rule of prayer?

After learning the Lord's Prayer, I should next aim to learn certain psalms *(such as Psalms 23, 51, 95, 100, 150)* and prayers from the Daily Office. These prayers will ground me in the Christian tradition of prayer and teach me how to pray in my own words.

242. What should you remember when prayers seem to go unanswered?

I should be certain that God always hears my prayers and answers them by his wisdom, in his own time and manner, for my good, and for his glory. *(Psalm 37:3–9; Isaiah 55; Habakkuk 3:17–19; Luke 18:1–8; James 4:2–3; 1 John 5:14–15)*

243. How should you pray in times of suffering?

I should pray trusting in the sufficiency of God's grace and in joyful assurance that "suffering produces endurance, and endurance produces character, and character produces hope, and hope does not put us to shame." *(Romans 5:3–5; see also Job 23; Psalm 22; John 12:23–26; 2 Corinthians 1:3–5; 1 Peter 4:12–19)*

CORPORATE WORSHIP

244. What is liturgy?

Liturgy is an established pattern or form for the worship of God by God's people. The liturgy leads us in the remembrance of God's mighty acts and unites us in grateful response. *(Exodus 15:1–21; Psalm 118; Luke 22:14–20; 1 Corinthians 11:23–26)*

245. Why do Anglicans worship with a structured liturgy?

Anglicans worship with a structured liturgy because it embodies biblical patterns of worship, fosters reverence and love for God, deepens faith in Jesus Christ, and is in continuity with the practices of Israel and the Early Church. *(Numbers 6:22–27; Deuteronomy 12:8–14; Psalm 96; Acts 2:42–47; Revelation 15; Didache 8–10)*

246. Does structured liturgy inhibit sincere and vibrant worship?

No. A structured liturgy provides sincere worshipers biblical language and forms that train our hearts for worship. Liturgy enables us to worship God joyfully and with one voice. *(2 Samuel 6:1–4; 2 Chronicles 29; Psalm 68:24–33; 1 Corinthians 14:26–33, 39–40; Revelation 7:9–8:5)*

247. What is the role of Scripture in the Prayer Book?

The Book of Common Prayer is saturated with the Scriptures, organizing and orchestrating them for worship. It helps us to pray together in words God himself has given us, with order, beauty, joy, deep devotion, and great dignity. *(Exodus 34:5–8; 1 Chronicles 29:10–13; Psalms 96:9; 118; Matthew 21:1–11; Revelation 7:9–12)*

248. How does the Book of Common Prayer organize corporate worship?

The Prayer Book orders our daily, weekly, and seasonal prayer and worship. It also provides liturgies for significant events of life. *(Leviticus 23:1–24:9; Psalm 90; John 2:1–12; 1 Corinthians 15:1–11)*

249. What is the Daily Office?

The Daily Office includes the services of Morning and Evening Prayer. In them we confess our sins and receive absolution, hear God's Word and praise him with psalms, and offer the Church's thanksgivings and prayers. *(Psalms 5; 63; Daniel 6:10; Mark 1:35)*

250. How is the Daily Office observed?

The Daily Office is primarily designed for corporate prayer. It may also be used by individuals or families, in public or in private, in whole or in part. *(Psalm 22:22–27; Acts 10:9–16; Hebrews 10:24–25; Revelation 7:9–12)*

251. **Why do we pray the Daily Office?**

We pray the Daily Office because, by it, we learn the Scriptures, join with the Church in prayer, mark our days with praise to God, and sanctify our time. *(Joshua 1:6–9; Psalms 92; 119:97; Acts 10:1–8; 1 Timothy 2:1–7)*

TOWARD A RULE OF LIFE

252. **What is a rule of life?**

A rule of life is a discipline by which I order my worship, work, and leisure as a pleasing sacrifice to God. *(Deuteronomy 6:1–9; Psalm 103; John 15:1–15; Romans 12:1–2; Colossians 3:12–17)*

253. **Why do you need a rule of life?**

I need a rule of life because my fallen nature is disordered, distracted, and self-centered. A rule of life helps me to resist sin and establish godly habits, through which the Holy Spirit will increasingly conform me to the image of Christ. *(Psalms 73; 86:11–13; Proverbs 3; 1 Corinthians 9:23–27; Colossians 3:1–4; 1 Peter 1:13–19)*

254. **What is included in a rule of life?**

In addition to Scripture, prayer, and worship, a rule of life includes witness, service, self-denial, and faithful stewardship of my time, money, and possessions. *(Deuteronomy 5:28–33; Psalm 141; Matthew 5:13–16; 6:19–24; Mark 8:27–38; 1 Peter 4:10–11)*

255. **Why is prayer an essential part of a rule of life?**

Through prayer, I rely upon God for strength, wisdom, and humility to sustain and guide me in my rule of life. Without the love of God and the power of his Spirit, I will not attain to the fullness of Christ. *(Job 28:12–28; Psalm 143; Romans 8:26–30)*

Concluding Prayer

Our Father, who art in heaven,
hallowed be thy Name,
thy kingdom come,
thy will be done,
on earth as it is in heaven.
Give us this day our daily bread.
And forgive us our trespasses,
as we forgive those
who trespass against us.
And lead us not into temptation,
but deliver us from evil.
For thine is the kingdom,
and the power, and the glory,
for ever and ever. **Amen.**

PART IV

BECOMING
LIKE CHRIST

Jesus Christ calls his disciples to respond to God in three basic ways: by believing in Jesus and God's revealed truth about him, by belonging to Jesus and communing with God through him, and by becoming like Jesus in doing God's will. The Holy Spirit enables us to respond to God in these ways.

God wants us to have fullness of life in a relationship of loving obedience to him. He teaches us his will for our lives through the Law, and most fully through the teaching and example of Jesus *(John 12:49–50; Hebrews 1:1–2)*. God's Law is outlined and distilled for us in the Ten Commandments, and displayed for us in Jesus' sinless life and atoning death.

Because God has created human beings in his image, the principles and standards of his Law are, to some degree, impressed upon the consciences of all people *(Romans 2:15)*. However, God gave his Law in a clear and direct way to his chosen people, Israel. Having delivered them from slavery in Egypt, he established a covenant relationship with them at Mount Sinai, giving them his Law through Moses with the Ten Commandments at its heart. God promised to bless Israel, and Israel vowed to worship and serve God only, by living as his holy people in grateful obedience to his will *(Exodus 19:5–6; 24:3)*.

Israel failed to keep God's Law, as do all human beings. However, God's Law was perfectly fulfilled in the sinless life and sacrificial death of his Son, Jesus, the Messiah. Through Jesus, God delivers us from slavery to sin and death, adopts us as his children, and establishes a new covenant with us. Thus, the Christian life of holiness is rooted in the gracious union that believers have with the Father, through the Son, and by the Holy Spirit.

Jesus summarizes the Law for us in his command to love God and our neighbor. His moral teaching unfolds the Law and applies it to the human heart. His teaching is universal, authoritative, and final. His ultimate goal is to conform us to his own likeness, that we too will be radiant with the holiness of God. Therefore, grateful obedience to the commandments of Jesus is an essential part of the life we have received through faith in him *(Matthew 28:20; John 14:15)*.

God's purpose for our new life in Christ is to make us like Jesus *(Romans 8:28–29)*. Scripture teaches that our actions are pleasing to God only if the attitudes of our minds and hearts are also godly. God sees our behavior as the "fruit" of our hearts and character, not as something external or separate from our inner being. Thus, the goal of our life in Christ is that we become like Christ—not only in our actions, but also in our thoughts and attitudes.

A Prayer for Spiritual Provision and Protection

Heavenly Father, you made us for yourself, and our hearts are restless until they rest in you: Look upon the heartfelt desires of your humble servants, and stretch forth the strong hand of your Majesty to be our defense against our enemies; through Jesus Christ our Lord; who lives and reigns with you and the Holy Spirit, world without end. **Amen.**

THE TEN COMMANDMENTS

256. Recite the Ten Commandments.
 1. I am the Lord your God. You shall have no other gods but me.
 2. You shall not make for yourself any idol.
 3. You shall not take the Name of the Lord your God in vain.
 4. Remember the Sabbath day and keep it holy.
 5. Honor your father and your mother.
 6. You shall not murder.
 7. You shall not commit adultery.
 8. You shall not steal.
 9. You shall not bear false witness against your neighbor.
 10. You shall not covet.
 (Book of Common Prayer 2019 version from Exodus 20:1–17; Deuteronomy 5:6–21)

257. What are the Ten Commandments?
The Ten Commandments are a summary and outline of God's Law. *(Exodus 20:18–21; Deuteronomy 5:28–33; Psalm 78:5–8)*

258. What is God's Law?
God's Law (Hebrew, *torah*: "instruction") is God's direct pronouncement of his will, both for our good and for his glory. *(Deuteronomy 30; Psalms 19:7–11; 119:89–104; Galatians 3:15–24)*

259. When did God give his Law?
After delivering his people Israel from slavery in Egypt, God established a covenant with them by giving them his Law through Moses. *(Exodus 19:1–6; Deuteronomy 5:1–5; Nehemiah 9:13–14; Acts 7:35–38)*

260. How did Jesus summarize God's Law?

Jesus summarized God's Law by saying: "You shall love the Lord your God with all your heart and with all your soul and with all your mind. This is the great and first commandment. And a second is like it: You shall love your neighbor as yourself. On these two commandments depend all the Law and the Prophets." *(Matthew 22:37–40; see also Deuteronomy 6:1–9; Leviticus 19:9–18; Psalm 31:23–24; John 15:7–17; 1 John 4:16–5:3)*

261. How did Jesus fulfill God's Law?

For our sake, Jesus fulfilled God's Law by teaching it perfectly, submitting to it wholly, and dying as an atoning sacrifice for our disobedience. *(Psalm 119:49–72; Isaiah 53:4–12; Matthew 5:17–20; Romans 8:1–4; Hebrews 10:1–18)*

262. How can you obey God's Law?

As I trust in Jesus' fulfillment of the Law for me and live in the power of the Holy Spirit, God grants me grace to love and obey his Law. *(2 Kings 18:1–8; Proverbs 3:1–12; John 15:3–11; Romans 6:15–23; 1 John 5:2–5)*

263. Why are you not able to do this perfectly?

Sin has corrupted human nature, inclining me to resist God, to ignore his will, and to care more for myself than for my neighbors. However, God has begun and will continue his transforming work in me, and will fully conform me to Christ at the end of the age. *(Psalm 14; Jeremiah 17:1–13; Romans 3:9–23; 7:21–25; Philippians 1:3–11)*

264. How should you understand the Ten Commandments?

I should understand them as God's righteous rules for life in his kingdom: basic standards for loving God and my neighbor. In upholding them, I bear witness with the Church to God's righteousness and his will for a just society. *(Deuteronomy 4:1–8; Psalm 119:137–44, 160; Matthew 5:17–48; Romans 7:7–12; 13:8–10)*

265. How do the Ten Commandments help you to resist evil?

They teach me that God judges the corrupt affections of this fallen world, the cruel strategies of the devil, and the sinful desires of my own heart; and they teach me to renounce them. *(Deuteronomy 8; Psalm 19:7–14; John 16:7–15; Romans 2:1–16)*

266. How do the Ten Commandments help you to grow in likeness to Christ?

They reveal my sin in the light of God's righteousness, guide me to Christ, and teach me what is pleasing to God. *(Deuteronomy 4:32–40; Psalms 19; 119:127–35, 169–76; Galatians 3:19–26; James 1:21–25; 2:8–13)*

267. How should you keep the Ten Commandments?

Because they both contain God's prohibitions against evil and direct me toward his good will, I should both repent when I disobey them and seek by his grace to live according to them. *(Psalm 25:11–18; Romans 6; Colossians 3:5–17)*

THE FIRST COMMANDMENT

268. What is the first commandment?

The first commandment is "I am the LORD your God. . . . You shall have no other gods before me." *(Exodus 20:2–3; Deuteronomy 5:6–7; see also Psalm 97; Luke 4:5–8; 1 Corinthians 8:1–6)*

269. What does it mean that the Lord is your God?

It means that I have faith that the God of the Bible is the only true God and that I entrust myself to him wholly. *(Exodus*

3:1–15; Deuteronomy 6:4–5; Psalm 86:8–13; Mark 12:29–34; Revelation 15:3–4)

270. What does it mean to have no other gods?

It means that there should be nothing in my life more important than God and obeying his will. I should worship him only and love, revere, and trust him above all else. *(Psalm 95; Jeremiah 10:6–10; Luke 16:10–15; 1 John 2:15–17)*

271. Why are you tempted to worship other things instead of God?

I am tempted because my sinful heart seeks my own desires above all else and pursues those things which falsely promise to fulfill them. *(Deuteronomy 29:16–19; Psalm 10:2–7; Acts 19:23–27; James 4:1–10)*

272. How are you tempted to worship other gods?

I am tempted to trust in myself, my pleasures, my possessions, my relationships, and my success, wrongly believing that they will bring me happiness, security, and meaning. I am also tempted to believe superstitions and false religious claims, and to reject God's call to worship him alone. *(1 Kings 11:1–8; Psalm 73:1–17; Matthew 26:14–16; 27:1–5; Romans 1:18–32)*

273. Can you worship and serve God perfectly?

No. Only our Lord Jesus Christ worshiped and served God perfectly; but I can seek to imitate Christ, knowing that my worship and service are acceptable to God through him. *(1 Kings 15:9–14; Psalm 53:1–3; Luke 4:1–13; Ephesians 5:1–2; Hebrews 7:23–28)*

THE SECOND COMMANDMENT

274. What is the second commandment?

The second commandment is "You shall not make for yourself a carved image, or any likeness of anything that is in heaven above, or that is in the earth beneath, or that is in the water under the earth. You shall not bow down to them or serve them." *(Exodus 20:4–6; 34:17; Deuteronomy 5:8–10)*

275. What does the second commandment mean?

God's people are neither to worship man-made images of God or of other gods nor to make such images for the purpose of worshiping them. *(Exodus 20:23; 34:17; Leviticus 26:1; Deuteronomy 4:15–20; 27:15; Psalm 97:6–9; Acts 17:22–29; 2 Corinthians 6:16–18)*

276. How did Israel break the first two commandments?

Israel neglected God's Law, worshiped the gods of the nations around them, and brought images of these gods (idols) into God's temple, thus corrupting his worship. *(Exodus 32; Judges 10:6; 1 Kings 12:28–33; 2 Kings 21:1–9; Psalm 106:19–43; Hosea 13:2; 1 Corinthians 10:1–14)*

277. Why did the nations make such images?

Israel's neighbors worshiped and served false gods by means of idols, believing they could manipulate these counterfeit gods for their own benefit. *(Psalm 115:2–8; Isaiah 44:9–20; Jeremiah 10:2–15; Habakkuk 2:18–19; Revelation 2:18–29)*

278. Are all images wrong?

No. God forbade the making of idols and the worship of images, yet commanded carvings and pictures for the tabernacle depicting creation. Christians are free to make images—including images of Jesus and the saints—as long as they do not worship them or use them superstitiously. *(Exodus 37:1–9; Numbers 21:4–9; 1 Kings 6:23–35; 7:23–26; John 3:9–15)*

279. Are idols always images?
No. Anything can become an idol if I look to it for salvation from my sin or comfort amid my circumstances. If I place my ultimate hope in anything but God, it is an idol. *(1 Samuel 15:23; Ezekiel 14:3–5; Ephesians 5:5; Colossians 3:5)*

280. What does the second commandment teach you about hope?
It teaches me that my ultimate hope is in God alone, for he alone is God and he made me. I must not look for salvation and fulfillment in myself, another person, my wealth or occupation or status, or any created thing. Only in God will I find perfect love and fulfillment. *(Psalm 62; Isaiah 45:20–25; Matthew 6:19–24; 1 Thessalonians 1:9–10)*

281. How was Jesus tempted to break the first two commandments?
Satan tempted Jesus to bow down and worship him, promising him an earthly kingdom without the pain of the Cross. Instead, Jesus served and worshiped God faithfully and perfectly all his life, and calls us to do the same. *(Matthew 4:1–11; 16:24; Luke 22:41–44; Philippians 2:8)*

282. How will idolatry affect you?
If I worship and serve idols, I will become like them, empty and alienated from God, who alone can make me whole. *(Psalm 115:4–8; Jeremiah 2:11–19; Jonah 2:7–9; Romans 1:18–25)*

THE THIRD COMMANDMENT

283. What is the third commandment?

The third commandment is "You shall not take the name of the LORD your God in vain." *(Exodus 20:7; Deuteronomy 5:11; see also Leviticus 22:32; see questions 172–77)*

284. Why is God's Name sacred?

God's Name reveals who he is—his nature, his character, his power, and his purposes. All forms of God's Name are holy. *(Exodus 3:1–15; 34:5–7; Psalms 8; 54:1; 79:9; Isaiah 57:15; Luke 1:46–49)*

285. What does it mean to take God's Name "in vain"?

"Vain" means empty, meaningless, and of no account. To take God's Name in vain is to treat it as such. *(Leviticus 24:10–16; Romans 2:23–24)*

286. How can you avoid taking God's Name in vain?

Because I love him, I should use God's Name with reverence, not carelessly or profanely. *(Deuteronomy 28:58–59; Psalms 86:11–12; 99:1–5; Revelation 15:2–4)*

287. How might you use God's Name profanely?

By the unholy use of God's holy Name, especially through perjury, blasphemy, and attributing to God any falsehood, heresy, or evil deed, as if he had authorized or approved them. *(Deuteronomy 18:20–22; Proverbs 30:7–9; Jeremiah 34:15–16; Ezekiel 36:16–23; Amos 2:6–7; Jude 5–13)*

288. How might you use God's Name carelessly?

Cursing, magic, broken vows, false piety, manipulation of others, and hypocrisy all cheapen God's Name. These treat God's Name as empty of the reality for which it stands. *(Leviticus 5:4–6; 19:26b, 31; Psalm 10:2–7; Malachi 1:6–14; Matthew 5:33–37; James 3:5–12; Articles of Religion, 39)*

289. How can you honor and love God's Name?

I honor and love God's Name, in which I was baptized, by keeping my vows and promises, by worshiping him in truth and holiness, and by invoking his Name reverently and responsibly. *(Numbers 30:2; Deuteronomy 10:20–22; Psalm 105:1–5; Matthew 15:10–20; James 5:12)*

THE FOURTH COMMANDMENT

290. What is the fourth commandment?

The fourth commandment is "Remember the Sabbath day, to keep it holy." *(Exodus 20:8–10; see also Deuteronomy 5:12–14)*

291. What does it mean to keep the Sabbath day holy?

"Sabbath" is from the Hebrew *shabbath*, which means "rest." "Holy" means "set apart" for God's purposes. God commanded Israel to set apart each seventh day, following six days of work, for rest and worship. *(Genesis 2:2; Exodus 31:12–17; Psalm 23:1–3; Mark 1:21–22)*

292. Why was Israel to rest on the Sabbath?

Israel was called to rest in remembrance that God had freed them from slavery and that God rested from his work of creation, bringing joyful balance and rhythm to life, work, and worship. *(Genesis 2:1–2; Exodus 20:11; 23:12; Deuteronomy 5:12–15)*

293. How did Jesus teach us to keep the Sabbath?

As Lord of the Sabbath, Jesus taught us to keep it not merely as a duty, but as a gift of God to be received with joy and extended to others through acts of love and hospitality. *(Mark 2:23–3:6; Luke 13:10–16)*

294. **How does the Sabbath serve as a promise for the future of God's people?**

When the Church is perfected in Christ, all believers will dwell in God's new creation, free from sin and its curse, and eternally united to God in love, adoration, and joy. This will be our unending Sabbath rest. *(Psalm 132; Isaiah 66:22–23; Colossians 2:16–19; Hebrews 4:1–13)*

295. **How do you keep the Sabbath?**

I cease from all unnecessary work; rest physically, mentally, and spiritually; and join with my family and church in worship, fellowship, and works of love. *(Psalm 92; Isaiah 58:13–14; Matthew 12:12; Colossians 2:16–23)*

296. **What does this commandment teach you about work?**

My work is a gift of God that can grant me provision and satisfaction, and serve the common good, but it neither defines my life nor rules over it. I am thereby freed from resentment and sloth to work diligently and with joy for God's glory. *(Genesis 2:15; Exodus 20:9–11; Psalm 128; Proverbs 6:6–11; 12:11–14; 16:3; Ephesians 4:28; Colossians 3:23–24)*

297. **Why does the Church worship on the first day of the week rather than the seventh?**

The earliest Christians came to observe Sunday as "the Lord's Day" *(Revelation 1:10)* for their primary day of worship in remembrance of Jesus' resurrection on the first day of the week. *(Luke 24:1–7; Acts 20:7; 1 Corinthians 16:2; Didache 14.1; Ignatius of Antioch, Letter to the Magnesians 9)*

298. What does the Sabbath teach you about time?

Through an ordered life of weekly worship and rest throughout the Christian year, and by a regular pattern of daily prayer, I learn that time belongs to God and is ordered by him. *(Genesis 1:14–15; Leviticus 23; Psalms 92:1–4; 119:164; Acts 3:1; Hebrews 10:25)*

299. How does keeping the Sabbath help you to grow in Christ?

As I keep a weekly day of rest and worship, my faith in God my Creator is strengthened, my hope in God my Provider is renewed, and my love for God my Redeemer is deepened. *(Exodus 16:1–30; Psalm 127:1–2; Hebrews 10:19–25)*

THE FIFTH COMMANDMENT

300. What is the Fifth commandment?

The fifth commandment is "Honor your father and your mother." *(Exodus 20:12; Deuteronomy 5:16)*

301. What does it mean to honor your father and mother?

I should love, serve, respect, and care for my parents all their lives, and should obey them in all things that are reasonable and conform to God's Law. *(Genesis 45:7–13; Proverbs 6:20–22; 20:20; 23:22; Ephesians 6:1–3; Colossians 3:20)*

302. How should parents treat their children?

Earthly fathers and mothers should represent to their children the loving care of our heavenly Father by nurturing and protecting them, teaching and modeling to them the Christian faith and life, guiding and assisting them in education, and encouraging them in their lives and vocations. *(Genesis 48:8–16; Deuteronomy 6:4–7; Proverbs 19:18; 22:6; Matthew 3:13–17; Ephesians 6:4; Colossians 3:21; 1 Timothy 5:8)*

303. **How did Jesus keep the fifth commandment?**

As a child, Jesus obeyed Joseph and Mary; on the Cross, he provided for his mother by entrusting her to his disciple's care; in his life, he obeyed the lawful requirements of the civil and religious authorities; and in all things he sought to do his Father's will. *(Luke 2:39–52; John 10:22–39; 19:25–27)*

304. **How else do you love God in light of the fifth commandment?**

I also keep the fifth commandment by showing respect for teachers and elders; by obeying, as far as is lawful, those who hold authority in the Church, my employment, and civil government; and by conducting myself in all things with reverent humility before God and my neighbor. *(Exodus 22:28; Matthew 22:15–22; Romans 13:1–7; 1 Timothy 2:1–2; 5:1–4; Hebrews 13:7; 1 Peter 2:13–15; Articles of Religion, 37)*

305. **What blessings result from obeying the fifth commandment?**

Submission to God's appointed earthly authorities helps me to resist pride and grow in humility, and promotes the justice and peace (*shalom*) of society in which human life flourishes. *(Exodus 20:12; 1 Chronicles 29:23; Proverbs 10:17; Romans 13:1–4; Hebrews 13:17)*

306. **Does earthly authority have limits?**

Yes. All authority comes from God, the King of kings, who expects me to love, honor, and obey him above all earthly authorities whenever they command me to sin. *(Exodus 1:15–21; Daniel 3:4–6, 16–18; Matthew 23:1–4; Acts 5:27–29; Revelation 18:1–4)*

THE SIXTH COMMANDMENT

307. **What is the sixth commandment?**

The sixth commandment is "You shall not murder." *(Exodus 20:13; Deuteronomy 5:17)*

308. What is murder?
Murder is the willful and unjust taking of human life. *(Genesis 4:1–10; Deuteronomy 19:4–13; Acts 7:54–8:3)*

309. Why does God prohibit murder?
Because every human being is made in God's image, all human life is sacred, from conception to natural death. Therefore, I may not take the life of others unjustly. *(Genesis 9:6; Deuteronomy 19:4–13; Psalm 94:1–7; Isaiah 46:3–4; Romans 12:19–21)*

310. What other actions are considered murder?
Genocide, infanticide, abortion, suicide, and euthanasia are all forms of murder. Sins of murderous intent include physical and emotional abuse, abandonment, willful negligence, and wanton recklessness. *(Exodus 1:15–22; 21:28–30; 2 Kings 17:16–18; Psalm 139:13–16; Amos 1:13–15; Acts 9:1–2; Didache 2.2)*

311. How did Jesus extend the law against murder?
Jesus taught that this commandment also forbids the vice of ungodly anger. A murderous heart can lead to hatred, threatening words, violent acts, and murder itself, and is counter to God's life-affirming love. *(Leviticus 19:17–18; Matthew 5:21–22, 43–45; 15:18–20; 1 John 3:15)*

312. Is anger always sinful?
While godly anger is a just response to wickedness and injustice, we are more often led into ungodly anger by fear, pride, and revenge. We should therefore be slow to anger and quick to forgive. *(Psalm 103:8–9; Proverbs 15:18; 16:32; 19:11; Micah 7:18; John 2:13–17; Ephesians 4:26–27, 31–32; James 1:19–20)*

313. Is it always wrong to harm or kill another?

There are circumstances in which justice, the protection of the weak and defenseless, and the preservation of life may require acts of violence. It is the particular task of government to uphold these principles in society. However, our Lord calls us to show mercy and to return evil with good. *(Numbers 35:9–34; Matthew 5:43–45; Romans 12:17–21; 13:1–4; Articles of Religion 37)*

314. How should Christians understand the value of life?

All life belongs to God. Human life is especially sacred because we are created in God's image, and because Jesus came to give us new and abundant life in him. Christians, therefore, should act with reverence toward all living things, and with special regard for the sanctity of human life. *(Genesis 1:26–27; 2:5–8; Psalm 104:24–30; Matthew 6:26; John 10:10; Acts 17:24–29; Colossians 1:15–20)*

315. How did Christ cause life to flourish?

Jesus sought the well-being of all who came to him: he healed the sick, fed the hungry, cast out demons, raised the dead, preached good news, forgave his enemies, and offered his life to redeem ours. *(Isaiah 53:4–5; Matthew 4:13–17; Luke 4:17–21; 7:20–22; 23:32–34; Acts 10:34–42)*

316. How else can you obey this commandment?

As a witness to the Gospel and a follower of Christ, I can also keep this commandment by forgiving those who wrong me, patiently refraining from ungodly anger and hateful words; defending the unborn, vulnerable, and oppressed; rescuing those who harm themselves; and seeking the well-being of all. *(Psalm 37:5–11; Zechariah 7:8–14; Matthew 5:38–48; Ephesians 4:25–5:2; James 1:27)*

THE SEVENTH COMMANDMENT

317. What is the seventh commandment?
The seventh commandment is "You shall not commit adultery." *(Exodus 20:14; Deuteronomy 5:18; see also Proverbs 6:32; Hebrews 13:4)*

318. What is adultery?
Adultery is any sexual intimacy between persons not married to each other, at least one of whom is married to another. *(Leviticus 20:10; Romans 7:2–3)*

319. What did Jesus teach about adultery?
Jesus taught that even to look at another person with lust violates this commandment. Adultery begins with a lustful heart, but the Lord calls us to be chaste. *(Matthew 5:27–28)*

320. What does it mean for you to be chaste?
Whether I am married or single, it means I will love and honor others as image bearers of God, not as objects of lust and sexual gratification, and I will refrain from all sexual acts outside of marriage. *(Genesis 39:6b–12; Proverbs 6:25–28; Matthew 5:29–30; Philippians 4:8; 1 Thessalonians 4:3–7)*

321. How do you benefit from chastity?
Chastity establishes wise and godly boundaries that enable me to give freely of myself in friendship, avoid difficulty in marriage, and experience the freedom of integrity before God. *(Genesis 39:19–23; Proverbs 11:5–6; Matthew 5:8; 1 Corinthians 7:25–40)*

322. What is marriage?
Marriage is the exclusive, lifelong, covenantal union of love between one man and one woman, and a reflection of the faithful love that unites God and his people. Marriage is therefore holy and should

"be held in honor among all." *(Hebrews 13:4; see also Genesis 2:18–24; Matthew 19:4–6; Ephesians 5:21–33; see questions 146–48)*

323. Why did God ordain marriage?

God ordained marriage for the procreation of children to be brought up in the nurture and admonition of the Lord; for a remedy against sin and to avoid sexual immorality; for mutual friendship, help, and comfort, both in prosperity and in adversity; and for the benefit of family, church, and society. *(Genesis 1:28; 2:18; Deuteronomy 6:4–9; 24:5; Psalm 127:3–5; Proverbs 31:10–12; 1 Corinthians 7:2–5; "Holy Matrimony," Book of Common Prayer 2019)*

324. Why does God forbid adultery?

Adultery is a sin against one's spouse or spouse-to-be; against the sexual partners with whom it is committed; against their children, family, and friends; against human society by undermining the institution of marriage; and against God, in whose Name marriage vows are made. *(2 Samuel 11:2–12:14; Proverbs 5; Malachi 2:13–16)*

325. What else did Jesus teach concerning this commandment?

Jesus also taught that divorce violates God's intention for marriage. *(Matthew 19:1–9; Mark 10:1–12)*

326. Is divorce ever permitted?

The New Testament permits divorce in some cases; however, out of love for his people, God hates divorce because it severs what he has joined, causes immeasurable pain, and destroys family life. *(Matthew 5:31–32; 19:7–9; 1 Corinthians 7:10–16)*

327. How should a single person keep the seventh commandment?

Those who are single should honor as holy their own bodies and those of others by refraining from sexual acts, lewd speech, or lustful thoughts. They should nurture chaste and loyal friendships, and uphold the common life of their families, fellowships, and churches. *(1 Corinthians 6:12–20; 7:6–9)*

328. Are some called to lifelong celibacy?
Yes. God calls some to an unmarried life of faithfulness and chastity. This calling enables them to devote their lives to God's service without the responsibilities of marriage and family. *(Matthew 19:10–12; 1 Corinthians 7:32–35)*

329. How else is the seventh commandment broken?
Violations of this law include sexual harassment and abuse, rape, incest, pedophilia, bestiality, same-sex sexual acts, prostitution, pornography, and any other form of lust in thought, word, or deed. *(Leviticus 18:6–30; Matthew 5:27–28; Romans 1:24–28)*

THE EIGHTH COMMANDMENT

330. What is the eighth commandment?
The eighth commandment is "You shall not steal." *(Exodus 20:15; Deuteronomy 5:19)*

331. What is stealing?
Stealing is the unauthorized and willful taking of what rightly belongs to another. *(Joshua 7:10–26; Proverbs 1:10–19; Luke 19:1–10; Acts 5:1–11)*

332. Why does God forbid stealing?
God is Creator and Lord of this world, and all things come from him. Therefore, I must never take what God has not entrusted to me. *(Exodus 23:19a; Leviticus 19:10–11a, 23–25; 1 Chronicles 29:14; Psalms 24:1–2; 50:7–12; Romans 13:9; Ephesians 4:28)*

333. How did God teach Israel to respect the property of others?

God required restitution when property was stolen or destroyed; and he forbade unjust loans and oppression of the poor. *(Exodus 21:33–22:15; Leviticus 25:35–37; Psalm 37:21–22)*

334. What things besides property can you steal?

I can steal or defraud others of wages, identity, credit, or intellectual property; cheat in school or on my taxes; or fail to pay my debts. I must repay and, to the best of my ability, restore what I have stolen. *(Exodus 23:8; Deuteronomy 24:10–15, 17–22; Proverbs 20:23; Jeremiah 22:13; Micah 6:11; James 5:4)*

335. What did Jesus teach about this commandment?

Jesus taught that I cannot serve God and be a slave to greed. I should seek first his will and rule, and trust that he will provide for my needs. *(Matthew 6:19–24; Luke 12:13–34)*

336. How does this commandment teach you to view your possessions?

God desires that I be content, responsible, and generous with what he has given me. Everything I own I hold in trust as God's steward, to cultivate and use for his glory and my neighbor's good. *(Genesis 1:28–31; Leviticus 25; Psalm 37:16; Proverbs 16:8; Luke 12:32–34; 1 Timothy 6:6–10; Hebrews 13:5; Articles of Religion, 38)*

337. As God's steward, how are you commanded to use your possessions?

As I am able, I should earn my own living, care for my dependents, and give to the poor. I should use all my possessions to the glory of God and the good of creation. *(Deuteronomy 15:11; Psalm 41:1; Proverbs 30:8–9; Isaiah 58:6–7; Matthew 25:14–30; Luke 14:13; Ephesians 4:28; 2 Thessalonians 3:6–12; 1 Timothy 6:17–19)*

338. **What is an appropriate standard of giving for you as a Christian?**

A "tithe," which is 10 percent of my income, is the minimum standard of giving for the work of God's Church and the spread of his kingdom; yet I should generously give of all that God has entrusted to me. *(Genesis 14:17–20; Leviticus 27:30–33; Deuteronomy 14:22–29; Malachi 3:6–12; Matthew 23:23; Luke 21:1–4; 2 Corinthians 9:6–7)*

THE NINTH COMMANDMENT

339. **What is the ninth commandment?**

The ninth commandment is "You shall not bear false witness against your neighbor." *(Exodus 20:16; Deuteronomy 5:20)*

340. **What is bearing false witness against your neighbor?**

It is to willfully communicate a falsehood about my neighbor, either in legal or in other matters, in order to misrepresent them. *(Deuteronomy 19:16–19; Psalm 109; Proverbs 12:17; Matthew 26:57–61)*

341. **Why does God forbid such false witness?**

Because it defames and wounds my neighbor, erodes my love of truth, disobeys my Lord Jesus, and aligns me with Satan, the father of lies. *(Psalm 52:1–5; Proverbs 25:18; Jeremiah 9:3–9; John 8:42–47)*

342. **How is false witness given in public life?**

Any willful misrepresentation of the truth in legal, civic, or business affairs bears false witness, rebels against God's will, and subverts God's justice. *(Exodus 23:1–3; Leviticus 6:1–7; Proverbs 11:1; 24:23–26, 28–29; Acts 6:8–15)*

343. **How is false witness given in respect to the teaching of the Church?**

All false or misleading teaching concerning the Christian faith bears false witness against the truth of God's Word and abuses the authority given by Christ to his Body. *(Deuteronomy 13; Matthew 24:3–14; 2 Peter 2:1–3; 1 John 2:18–27)*

344. **What other acts are forbidden by this commandment?**

This commandment forbids all lying, slander, or gossip; all manipulative, deceitful, or insulting speech; and testifying falsely about myself for personal gain. *(Leviticus 19:15–17; Psalm 12:2–3; Proverbs 10:18; 11:12; 16:28; Matthew 5:21–22; Romans 16:17–18; 1 Peter 2:1)*

345. **What sort of speech should you practice instead?**

I should speak at all times with love, wisdom, and truth, so that my words may honor God, and comfort and encourage my neighbor. *(Psalm 32:2; Proverbs 12:17–20; 14:25; 15:1–4; Zechariah 8:16–17; Matthew 5:33–37; Ephesians 4:25)*

346. **When is it right to speak of your neighbor's sins?**

I am forbidden to gossip or slander, but I must speak the truth in love, reporting crime, speaking against injustice, and advocating for the helpless. *(Leviticus 19:17–18; Proverbs 28:23; 31:8–9; Matthew 18:15–17; Ephesians 4:15–16; James 5:19–20)*

347. **Must you always speak the whole truth?**

To keep a confidence or to protect the innocent, I may at times need to withhold the whole truth; and I should always exercise discretion, that my candor may not needlessly cause harm. *(Exodus 1:15–21; Joshua 2:1–14; Proverbs 11:13)*

348. **How does keeping this commandment help you to become like Christ?**

By practicing love and truthfulness in speech, I grow in self-restraint, kindness, and honesty, so that I may know God with a mind free of deception, praise him with an undefiled tongue, and more truly love my neighbor. *(Proverbs 8:1–17; Matthew 15:10–20; Ephesians 5:1–4; James 3:1–12)*

THE TENTH COMMANDMENT

349. **What is the tenth commandment?**

The tenth commandment is "You shall not covet . . . anything that is your neighbor's." *(Exodus 20:17; Deuteronomy 5:21)*

350. **What does it mean to covet?**

Coveting is the disordered desire for what belongs to another or what I am unable to have by law, by gift, or by right. *(Joshua 7:1, 10–26)*

351. **What does the tenth commandment forbid you to covet?**

It forbids me to covet my neighbor's property, possessions, relationships, or status, or anything else that is my neighbor's. *(Exodus 20:17; Deuteronomy 5:21; Job 31:7–12, 24–28)*

352. **Why does God forbid coveting?**

God forbids coveting because it breeds enmity with my neighbor, makes me captive to ungodly desire, and leads me into further sins. *(Deuteronomy 7:25; Proverbs 12:12; Ephesians 5:5; James 4:2)*

353. **Why do you covet?**

I covet because I do not trust God to provide what I need, and I do not remain content with what I have; rather, I persist in envy and desire. *(Proverbs 14:30; 23:17–18; Luke 12:13–21; Galatians 5:17–21)*

354. How can covetousness lead to other sins?

Covetousness begins with discontent and, as it grows in the heart, can lead to sins such as idolatry, adultery, and theft. *(2 Samuel 11; 1 Kings 21:1–19; Proverbs 1:8–19; James 1:14–15)*

355. What did Jesus teach about this commandment?

Jesus taught us not to seek anxiously after possessions, but to put our trust in God; and he showed us how to live by taking the form of a servant, and loving and trusting his Father in all things. *(Matthew 6:19–34; Acts 8:9–24; Philippians 2:3–11)*

356. How can you keep this commandment?

I can keep this commandment by learning contentment: seeking first the kingdom of God, meditating on God's provision in creation and in my life, cultivating gratitude for what I have and simplicity in what I want, and practicing joyful generosity toward others. *(Exodus 35:20–29; 36:2–5; Psalms 104; 145:15–21; Ecclesiastes 5:10; 2 Corinthians 9:6–15; 1 Timothy 6:6–10; Hebrews 13:5)*

JUSTIFICATION AND SANCTIFICATION: LIVING IN FORGIVENESS AND HEALING

357. Is it possible for you to keep these commandments?

No. I fail to keep them perfectly, however hard I try. They show me my inability to obey God's Law and my need for God's grace in Christ Jesus. *(1 Kings 8:46; Psalms 53:2–3; 130:3; Proverbs 20:9; Ecclesiastes 7:20; Romans 3:9–20; 1 John 1:8, 10)*

358. **Since you cannot perfectly keep God's Law, what has Jesus done on your behalf?**

As the perfect human and unblemished Lamb of God, Jesus lived a wholly obedient and sinless life. He suffered death for my redemption upon the Cross, offering himself once for all as a "full, perfect, and sufficient sacrifice, oblation, and satisfaction for the sins of the whole world." *("Holy Communion, Anglican Standard Text," Book of Common Prayer 2019; see also Isaiah 53:4–6; Mark 10:45; John 1:29; Romans 8:3–4; Colossians 2:13–15; Hebrews 10:10–14)*

359. **What do you receive through Christ's sacrifice?**

I receive the unmerited gift of God's grace. If I confess my sins, God grants me forgiveness and pardon through Christ's blood shed for me. *(Psalm 32:1–2; Isaiah 53:10–11; John 3:16–18; 2 Corinthians 5:19–21; Hebrews 9:11–15; 1 John 1:8–9; 2:1–2)*

360. **How does God enable you to live in his forgiveness?**

Through faith, repentance, and Baptism, I am made a member of Christ, a child of God, and an heir of the kingdom of heaven. Washed of sin and united to Christ, I am "justified," being declared righteous by God, and I am given the grace to live continually in repentance and faith. *(Psalm 130:4; John 15:26–16:1; Acts 22:16; Romans 5:12–21; Titus 3:3–8)*

361. **Does God's forgiveness excuse you from personal obedience?**

No. God has reconciled me to himself and freed me from bondage to sin in order to conform me to the image of his Son. As I live each day in gratitude for God's forgiveness, I seek to turn from sin and follow Christ in loving obedience. *(John 14:15–24; Romans 6:1–14; 2 Corinthians 5:14–15; 1 John 3:4–10)*

362. **Are you still affected by your sin, despite God's forgiveness?**
Yes. My sinful actions can harm my relationship with God, do lasting damage to others, and leave me conflicted within myself. I live in constant need of Christ's healing grace. *(2 Samuel 12:1–23; Psalm 32:1–5; Matthew 15:18–20; Romans 7:15–25; 1 Corinthians 10:1–13; 1 Thessalonians 4:1–8)*

363. **How does Jesus heal you?**
Through the gift of the Holy Spirit, as I continue in repentance and faith, Jesus mends my disordered soul from the effects of sin in my mind, will, and desires. *(2 Chronicles 7:12–14; Psalms 25:4–11; 41:4; 103:1–5; 2 Corinthians 3:17–18)*

364. **What is this healing called?**
This healing is called "sanctification," which means to be made whole and holy. By the work of the Holy Spirit, my mind, will, and desires are increasingly transformed and conformed to the character of Jesus Christ. *(Proverbs 2; John 17:15–17; Romans 12:1–2; 1 Corinthians 6:9–11; Ephesians 2:1–10; 3:14–21)*

365. **How does the Church assist in your sanctification?**
The Church's joyful worship, faithful teaching, grace-filled sacraments, Gospel-shaped calendar, compassionate ministry, loving discipline, and caring fellowship all assist my growth in Christ and are channels of God's abundant care for my soul. *(Ephesians 4:1–16; Philippians 3:12–21)*

366. **How does the Lord's Supper assist in your sanctification?**
In the Lord's Supper or Holy Eucharist, I hear the Law read, receive God's good news of forgiveness, recall my baptismal promises, have my faith renewed, and receive the grace of the Body and

Blood of Christ to continue following him in love and obedience. *(John 6:53–58; 1 Corinthians 10:15–16)*

367. For what does sanctification prepare you?

Sanctification enables me to serve and bear witness to Christ in this life, and prepares me for the glory of God in the world to come. There I will be completely freed from sin and conformed to the likeness of my Lord, whom I will see face-to-face. *(Matthew 5:16; 1 Corinthians 13:9–13; 2 Corinthians 3:17–18; 1 John 3:1–3)*

368. What marks a life of sanctification?

God calls me to a life marked by gratitude and joy. In gratitude for God's grace in Jesus, I die daily to the desires of my fallen nature. In the joy of knowing that I will become like Jesus, I live each day in service to him. *(Luke 9:23–26; Romans 5:1–5; 2 Corinthians 4:5–18; 1 Thessalonians 1:6–10; Titus 2:11–14)*

A Prayer for Increase in the Love of God

O God, you have prepared for those who love you such good things as surpass our understanding: Pour into our hearts such love towards you, that we, loving you in all things and above all things, may obtain your promises, which exceed all that we can desire; through Jesus Christ our Lord; who lives and reigns with you and the Holy Spirit, one God, for ever and ever. **Amen.**

PRAYERS
FOR USE WITH
THE CATECHISM

Prayer is an essential component in the catechetical process. It invites catechists, catechumens, and sponsors to participate in the presence and power of God, who is at work transforming disciples into the image of Jesus Christ. It is a vital means by which Christian faith moves beyond our heads into our hearts and hands, so that the reign of God will increase in and through us. Catechists and sponsors are encouraged to pray with and for catechumens during sessions, and to begin and end each session with prayer.

One classic type of prayer is the *collect* (pronounced 'kä-lekt). Collects capture a specific spiritual theme, sum it up, and bring it before the face of God, asking for his attention and response. The word "collect" comes from the task and action of the officiant/ celebrant in *collecting* all the prayers of the faithful at an event in which the specific theme is in focus. Collects are at once deeply theological yet simple in construction. They are designed to be poetic and memorable, so as to captivate both head and heart, turning them toward God.

Many of the following collects date to the first centuries of the Church. At the time of the Reformation, Archbishop Thomas Cranmer sensed a pastoral duty to restore understanding of the collects by translating many of them into the language of the people. In doing so, he elevated the central role of the Scriptures in Christian prayer and worship, for the collects are filled with many biblical words and phrases. Cranmer himself also produced many memorable prayers of poetic beauty and godly sensibility.

By learning these collects, catechumens are trained to think and pray in a deeply biblical and theological way. The following classic prayers of the Church are categorized by topic to help in the process of formation:

For repentance and forgiveness

Almighty and everlasting God, you hate nothing you have made, and you forgive the sins of all who are penitent: Create and make in us new and contrite hearts, that we, worthily lamenting our sins and acknowledging our wretchedness, may obtain of you, the God of all mercy, perfect remission and forgiveness; through Jesus Christ our Lord; who lives and reigns with you and the Holy Spirit, one God, for ever and ever. **Amen.**

For purity

Almighty God, to you all hearts are open, all desires known, and from you no secrets are hid: Cleanse the thoughts of our hearts by the inspiration of your Holy Spirit, that we may perfectly love you, and worthily magnify your holy Name; through Christ our Lord. **Amen.**

For transformation

O God, who wonderfully created, and yet more wonderfully restored, the dignity of human nature: Grant that we may share the divine life of him who humbled himself to share our humanity, your Son Jesus Christ our Lord; who lives and reigns with you, in the unity of the Holy Spirit, one God, for ever and ever. **Amen.**

For growth in the knowledge and love of God the Father

Almighty God, you so loved the world that you gave your only Son, that whoever believes in him would not perish but have eternal life: Pour into our hearts that most excellent gift of love by your Holy Spirit, that we may delight in the inheritance that is ours as your sons and daughters, and live to your praise and glory, through Jesus Christ. **Amen.**

Or

Heavenly Father, you have made us for yourself, and our hearts are restless until they rest in you: Look with compassion upon the heartfelt desires of your servants, and purify our disordered affections, that we may behold your eternal glory in the face of Christ Jesus; who lives and reigns with you and the Holy Spirit, one God, for ever and ever. **Amen.**

Or

O God, you have prepared for those who love you such good things as surpass our understanding: Pour into our hearts such love towards you, that we, loving you in all things and above all things, may obtain your promises, which exceed all that we can desire; through Jesus Christ our Lord; who lives and reigns with you and the Holy Spirit, one God, for ever and ever. **Amen.**

For growth in the knowledge of Christ

Almighty God, whom truly to know is everlasting life: Grant us so perfectly to know your Son Jesus Christ to be the way, the truth, and the life, that we may steadfastly follow his steps in the way that leads to eternal glory; through Jesus Christ your Son our Lord; who lives and reigns with you, in the unity of the Holy Spirit, one God, for ever and ever. **Amen.**

For rebirth and renewal in Christ

Almighty God, you have given your only-begotten Son to take our nature upon him, and to be born of a pure virgin: Grant that we, who have been born again and made your children by adoption and grace, may daily be renewed by your Holy Spirit; through our Lord Jesus Christ, to whom with you and the same Spirit be honor and glory, now and forever. **Amen.**

For growth in the Holy Spirit

O God, because without you we are not able to please you, mercifully grant that your Holy Spirit may in all things direct and rule our hearts; through Jesus Christ our Lord; who lives and reigns with you and the Holy Spirit, one God, now and forever. **Amen.**

Or

Heavenly Father, send your Holy Spirit into our hearts, to direct and rule us according to your will, to comfort us in all our afflictions, to defend us from all error, and to lead us into all truth; through Jesus Christ our Lord. **Amen.**

Or

O God, who taught the hearts of your faithful people by sending to them the light of your Holy Spirit: Grant us by the same Spirit to have a right judgment in all things, and evermore to rejoice in his holy comfort; through Jesus

Christ your Son our Lord; who lives and reigns with you, in the unity of the Holy Spirit, one God, for ever and ever. **Amen.**

For self-dedication and commitment to God's will

Almighty and eternal God, so draw our hearts to you, so guide our minds, so fill our imaginations, so control our wills, that we may be wholly yours, utterly dedicated to you; and then use us, we pray, as you will, and always to your glory and the welfare of your people; through our Lord and Savior Jesus Christ. **Amen.**

For guidance

Direct us, O Lord, in all our doings with your most gracious favor, and further us with your continual help; that in all our works begun, continued, and ended in you, we may glorify your holy Name, and finally, through your mercy, obtain everlasting life; through Jesus Christ our Lord. **Amen.**

For studying the Scriptures

Blessed Lord, who caused all holy Scriptures to be written for our learning: Grant us so to hear them, read, mark, learn, and inwardly digest them, that by patience and the comfort of your holy Word we may embrace and ever hold fast the blessed hope of everlasting life, which you have given us in our Savior Jesus Christ; who lives and reigns with you and the Holy Spirit, one God, for ever and ever. **Amen.**

For quiet hearts

O God of peace, who has taught us that in returning and rest we shall be saved, in quietness and in confidence shall be our strength: By the might of your Spirit lift us, we pray, to your presence, where we may be still and know that you are God; through Jesus Christ our Lord. **Amen.**

For protection

Visit this place, O Lord, and drive far from it all snares of the Enemy; let your holy angels dwell with us to preserve us in peace; and let your blessing be upon us always; through Jesus Christ our Lord. **Amen.**

Or

O God, the King eternal, whose light divides the day from the night and turns the shadow of death into the morning: Drive far from us all wrong desires, incline our hearts to keep your law, and guide our feet into the way of peace; that, having done your will with cheerfulness during the day, we may, when night comes, rejoice to give you thanks; through Jesus Christ our Lord. **Amen.**

In preparation for Baptism

Almighty God, by our baptism into the death and resurrection of your Son Jesus Christ, you turn us from the old life of sin: Grant that we, being reborn to new life in him, may live in righteousness and holiness all our days; through Jesus Christ our Lord, who lives and reigns with you and the Holy Spirit, one God, now and forever. **Amen.**

In preparation for Confirmation

Grant, Almighty God, that we, who have been redeemed from the old life of sin by our baptism into the death and resurrection of your Son Jesus Christ, may be filled with your Holy Spirit, and live in righteousness and true holiness; through Jesus Christ our Lord, who lives and reigns with you and the Holy Spirit, one God, now and forever. **Amen.**

For the ministry of sharing the Gospel with others

Lord Jesus Christ, you stretched out your arms of love on the hard wood of the Cross that everyone might come within the reach of your saving embrace: So clothe us in your Spirit that we, reaching forth our hands in love, may bring those who do not know you to the knowledge and love of you; for the honor of your Name. **Amen.**

A RITE FOR ADMISSION OF CATECHUMENS

This form is to be used for adults, or older children who are able to answer for themselves, at the beginning of a course of instruction in the teachings of the Church. It is to be used in preparation for Holy Baptism or, if those seeking admission were baptized as infants, for Confirmation.

GREETING

On the day appointed, the persons to be received as Catechumens are brought by their sponsors to the church and remain by the principal door until the Gospel has been proclaimed.

The Celebrant greets them at the door.

Celebrant	What is your hope?
Catechumens	**New life in Christ.**
Celebrant	What do you desire of God and of this congregation?
Catechumens	**That I may grow in faith, hope, and love.**

Then the Celebrant says,

If you hope to enter into eternal life, you must, by his grace, follow in our Lord's steps, for he said: "If anyone would come after me, let him deny himself and take up his cross and follow me."

EXAMINATION

Will you turn to Jesus Christ and accept him as your Lord and
Savior?
I will, with God's help.

As none can do this without God's grace, found in Word and
Sacrament, will you join with us in our common life of worship,
teaching, service, and fellowship?
I will.

ENROLLMENT AND EXORCISM

*The Celebrant leads them to the chancel steps, where they kneel, and the Celebrant
prays over them, saying,*

Let us pray.

O Lord God of hosts, before the terrors of whose presence the
armies of Hell are put to flight: Deliver *these* your *servants* from
the powers of the world, the flesh, and the Devil; cast out from
them every evil and unclean spirit that lurks in the heart, and any
spirit of error or wickedness; and make them ready to receive
the fullness of the Holy Spirit; through Jesus Christ our Lord.
Amen.

*The Celebrant then makes the sign of the Cross upon the forehead of each one (and
may use the Oil of Catechumens to do so), saying to each,*

Almighty God deliver you from the powers of darkness and evil
and lead you into the light and obedience of the kingdom of his
Son, Jesus Christ, our Lord. **Amen.**

THE BLESSING

The Catchumens all kneeling, the Celebrant then blesses them, saying,

Almighty God, who in his love for you has called you to the knowledge of his grace, grant you an entrance into his kingdom; through Jesus Christ, our Lord. **Amen.**

Sponsors accompany Catechumens to seats among the people.
The service continues with the Sermon and Nicene Creed.

APPENDIX 3

THE NICENE CREED

We believe in one God,
    the Father, the Almighty,
    maker of heaven and earth,
    of all that is, visible and invisible.

We believe in one Lord, Jesus Christ,
    the only-begotten Son of God,
    eternally begotten of the Father,
    God from God, Light from Light,
    true God from true God,
    begotten, not made,
    of one Being with the Father;
    through him all things were made.
    For us and for our salvation he came down from heaven,
    was incarnate from the Holy Spirit and the Virgin Mary,
    and was made man.
    For our sake he was crucified under Pontius Pilate;
    he suffered death and was buried.
    On the third day he rose again in accordance with the
        Scriptures;
    he ascended into heaven
    and is seated at the right hand of the Father.
    He will come again in glory to judge the living and
        the dead,
    and his kingdom will have no end.

We believe in the Holy Spirit, the Lord, the giver of life,
who proceeds from the Father [and the Son],[†]
who with the Father and the Son is worshiped and
glorified,
who has spoken through the prophets.
We believe in one holy catholic and apostolic Church.
We acknowledge one baptism for the forgiveness of sins.
We look for the resurrection of the dead,
and the life of the world to come. Amen.
(Book of Common Prayer 2019)

---

† The phrase "and the Son" (Latin, *filioque*) is not in the original Greek text. See the resolution of
the Anglican Church in North America College of Bishops concerning the *filioque* in *Documentary
Foundations* (page 768, Book of Common Prayer 2019).

THE CREED OF SAINT ATHANASIUS

Whosoever will be saved, before all things it is necessary
that he hold the Catholic Faith.

Which Faith except everyone do keep whole and undefiled,
without doubt he shall perish everlastingly.

And the Catholic Faith is this: That we worship one God in
Trinity, and Trinity in Unity, neither confounding the
Persons, nor dividing the Substance.

For there is one Person of the Father, another of the Son,
and another of the Holy Ghost.

But the Godhead of the Father, of the Son, and of the
Holy Ghost, is all one, the Glory equal, the Majesty
co-eternal.

Such as the Father is, such is the Son, and such is the Holy
Ghost.

The Father uncreate, the Son uncreate, and the Holy Ghost
uncreate.

The Father incomprehensible, the Son incomprehensible,
and the Holy Ghost incomprehensible.

The Father eternal, the Son eternal, and the Holy Ghost
eternal.

And yet they are not three eternals, but one eternal.

As also there are not three incomprehensibles, nor three
uncreated, but one uncreated, and one incomprehensible.

So likewise the Father is Almighty, the Son Almighty, and
the Holy Ghost Almighty.

And yet they are not three Almighties, but one Almighty.

So the Father is God, the Son is God, and the Holy Ghost
is God.

And yet they are not three Gods, but one God.

So likewise the Father is Lord, the Son Lord, and the Holy
Ghost Lord.

And yet not three Lords, but one Lord.

For like as we are compelled by the Christian verity to
acknowledge every Person by himself to be both God
and Lord,

So are we forbidden by the Catholic Religion, to say, There
be three Gods, or three Lords.

The Father is made of none, neither created, nor begotten.

The Son is of the Father alone, not made, nor created, but
begotten.

The Holy Ghost is of the Father and of the Son, neither
made, nor created, nor begotten, but proceeding.

So there is one Father, not three Fathers; one Son, not three
Sons; one Holy Ghost, not three Holy Ghosts.

And in this Trinity none is afore, or after other; none is
greater, or less than another;

But the whole three Persons are co-eternal together and
co-equal.

So that in all things, as is aforesaid, the Unity in Trinity and
the Trinity in Unity is to be worshipped.

He therefore that will be saved must think thus of the Trinity.

Furthermore, it is necessary to everlasting salvation that he also
believe rightly the Incarnation of our Lord Jesus Christ.

For the right Faith is, that we believe and confess, that our
Lord Jesus Christ, the Son of God, is God and Man;

God, of the substance of the Father, begotten before the
worlds; and Man of the substance of his Mother,
born in the world;

Perfect God and perfect Man, of a reasonable soul and
   human flesh subsisting.
Equal to the Father, as touching his Godhead; and inferior
   to the Father, as touching his manhood;
Who, although he be God and Man, yet he is not two, but
   one Christ;
One, not by conversion of the Godhead into flesh but by
   taking of the Manhood into God;
One altogether; not by confusion of Substance, but by unity
   of Person.
For as the reasonable soul and flesh is one man, so God and
   Man is one Christ;
Who suffered for our salvation, descended into hell, rose
   again the third day from the dead.
He ascended into heaven, he sitteth at the right hand of the
   Father, God Almighty, from whence he will come to
   judge the quick and the dead.
At whose coming all men will rise again with their bodies
   and shall give account for their own works.
And they that have done good shall go into life everlasting;
   and they that have done evil into everlasting fire.
This is the Catholic Faith, which except a man believe
   faithfully, he cannot be saved.[†]

---

† James Sullivan, "The Athanasian Creed," in *The Catholic Encyclopedia*, vol. 2 (New York: Robert Appleton, 1907), June 21, 2019, <http://www.newadvent.org/cathen/02033b.htm>.

APPENDIX 5

A NOTE ON THE ARTICLES OF RELIGION

Among the Fundamental Declarations set forth in its Constitution, the Anglican Church in North America has received the Thirty-Nine Articles of Religion of 1563/1571 (the "Articles of Religion"), taken in their literal and grammatical sense, as expressing the Anglican response to certain doctrinal issues controverted at that time, as expressing fundamental principles of authentic Anglican belief, and as one of the elements characteristic of the Anglican Way. In its Fundamental Declarations the Anglican Church in North America is determined by the help of God to hold and maintain, as the Anglican Way has received them, the doctrine, discipline, and worship of Christ and to transmit the same, unimpaired, to our posterity.

The Articles of Religion may be found in the "Documentary Foundations" of the Book of Common Prayer of the Anglican Church in North America.

The Constitution of the Anglican Church in North America may be accessed online at http://www.anglicanchurch.net/index.php/main/Governance/.

VISION PAPER FOR CATECHESIS

ANGLICAN CHURCH IN NORTH AMERICA

This important paper by the Committee for Catechesis provides a basic vision and outline for the process and content of catechesis in the Anglican Church in North America. Access it online at http://anglicanchurch.net/?/main/catechism.

APPENDIX 7

GUIDING PRINCIPLES FOR CATECHESIS

ANGLICAN CHURCH IN NORTH AMERICA

This document was produced by the Committee for Catechesis of the Anglican Church in North America (ACNA). Access it at http://anglicancatechism.com.

It presents a working definition of *catechesis* and the *catechumenate*, together with guiding principles for implementing this disciple-making initiative.

A mission-minded *dual* catechetical approach is set forth in the document: (1) catechetical evangelism—which focuses on disciple-making in an evangelistic situation (*from the "front porch" of the church*)—and (2) liturgical catechesis—which focuses on disciple-making within the formational contexts of family and church (*"from the font"*).

These principles are drawn from Anglican formularies and historic patterns from the undivided Church, and reflect a comprehensive framework for implementation. It is important that they be understood by those engaged in the task of catechesis.

INDEX OF SCRIPTURE